REDEEMING EVE

REDEEMING EVE

The Spirit, Not Gender, Determines Gifting in the Church.

Jim Reynolds

ISBN-13: 9780692555071
ISBN-10: 0692555072

Table of Contents

Acknowledgements

I am indebted to the Lake Highlands Church for being a Spirit-led church where the gifts have been embodied for a long time. Within this church environment, disciples are being mobilized for service in the church and the world. That mobilization includes women who have been doing the works God has gifted them to do. This happened in a real church at a local address. Without such a place, none of the truth regarding God's liberation and empowering of women would have been lived out. The witness of twenty-five years would not exist and this book would not have been written.

I thank all those church members who have been humble, kind, and longsuffering, and who preserved the unity of the Spirit in the bond of peace as we walked into the freedom Christ brings. This book is a witness to what God has done and is doing in a specific local church.

I also thank the women in the church – Kerri Reynolds, Diann Garnett, Donjalea Chrane, Robin Russell, and Jessica Lee, to name a few – who have quietly and faithfully pastored men and women in the church for the last fifteen years. Their gifted servant leadership has blessed the church. Clearly they are called, empowered, and equipped by the Spirit.

Mike King, a beloved friend and fellow elder, has read this manuscript more than once; his corrections and comments have made it a better manuscript. I am indebted to him for his friendship, encouragement, professional expertise, and living faith. I am also indebted to him for his spiritual discernment as to what God is doing in women. For more than two decades, his strong, calm voice has given more direction to me and the entire church than he knows.

Robin Russell, a professional editor-writer and a member of the church, has edited this book. I would be lost without her friendship, insights, and professional expertise. Because she is walking out the Way of Jesus as a woman in the Lake Highlands Church, her input goes way beyond her professionalism. She embodies the theological vision of this book and therefore knows the significance of the issues discussed. Thanks to her for her patience and kindness toward the church-at-large, which for many years ignored what God was doing through her. Hopefully that oversight is being corrected so that the body of Christ will be increasingly blessed by her gifts in the days ahead. There would be no book worth printing without her.

This book is a call for the church to reexamine the place of women in the True Story of the world as told in Scripture, and their place in church and society.

For more than six decades I have been patient – long-suffering is more accurate – with the oppression of women in the church, as have thousands of women I have known. I did not leave the church. I have not been arrogant or rude to those I consider dead wrong. But as a spiritual father in the church, there is a time to wait – and I have done that my entire life – and there is a time to say, "No more." That time is now.

For almost a quarter of a century I have listened to the testimony of the Spirit in the Lake Highlands Church and I am not going to say "no" any longer to what the Spirit is doing. That testimony weighs heavy now when discerning judgments must be made. There is no reason at this time in the life of the church to continue gender-based ministry in any form. It is time to claim the freedom of the Lord.

I came to the conclusions set out in this book twenty years before I recently read Dallas Willard's conclusions expressed in 2016, a few months before his death:

> Those gifted by the Spirit for any ministry should serve in the capacities enabled by the gift and human arrangements should facilitate their service and provide them the opportunities to serve. ... You have to put the fact that in discussing the

distribution and ministry of gifts of the Spirit, nothing is said about gender, alongside the fact that many men who manifestly are not supernaturally gifted are allowed to serve in leadership roles. Then you realize that official leadership roles, as widely understood now, are as much human artifacts as they are a divine arrangement.[1]

I have tried to make theological sense out of the way we disempower women, beginning with the silencing of my gifted mother as a youth pastor on the grounds that baptized boys in her classes were now men and were not to be instructed by a female teacher. I have endured teaching from ungifted males all my life in the church. Why is it we were always looking for men without gifts to do work that women were often gifted to do? At first it was just a bore; then it became an embarrassing tragedy.

When I entered Southern Methodist University's law school in 1978, it was filling up with women. They made up nearly half of the student body. Female judges and lawyers were everywhere. We were all placing ourselves under the authority of female judges every day. Women were running for President and the United States Senate. The patriarchal culture that had dominated Western culture from the days of the apostle Paul through the first seventy-five years of the 20th century was passing away. Now in 2014, we live in a culture that does not understand or respect the church's treatment of women.

I began asking myself new questions: if women are inferior and should never speak or bear any authority then why were Christians voting for women and placing themselves under female authority in the world but not in the church? How can what is right for Christians in the public square remain somehow wrong in the church?

For the last forty years the world has been doing for women what the church should have been doing all along. Mythologies about the inferiority of women were being shattered every day in law school and the courtroom yet were being repeated in the church. This double standard practiced by Christians did not pass the smell test. In fact I could not formulate a biblical defense of it. Given the fact that Jesus came to set the captives free, how is it that Christian men and women live together in society as equals under God but in Christ's body women are second-class citizens?

Christian women are writing books about Scripture, faith, and discipleship – and we are reading them. They have been teaching us for a long time. So is it a sin for a woman to teach men in person but not through the written word?

The ferment all around me has prompted the Spirit's moving within me to walk more fully in line with the truth of the gospel regarding the place of women in the church. Part of that walk is a reassessment of what Scripture says about women. That reassessment is coupled with a retelling of the story of women in the church tradition. I do not claim infallibility as to my convictions on this matter. I recognize that this issue is in part a theological interpretive issue; a disputable matter. There is no perfect, infallible way to interpret Scripture; having said that, we can simply do better because in our heart of hearts we know better. Failure to do better is to sin against the Lord God and women.

INTERPRETIVE DECISIONS AND OPPRESSION

As the Spirit has worked in the Lake Highlands Church over the last thirty years we have reexamined the ways we had interpreted Scripture that had led us to oppressive conclusions for women. These interpretive decisions were not directly related to women in the church but ultimately led us into a dead end as to women's role.

Our study revealed a systematic disempowerment of women, in part because we did not put the story of women into the True Story of the world, which begins in Genesis 1:1. Instead we jumped in 860 pages into the New International Version Bible and quoted passages that were thousands of years into the story, namely Paul's first letter to Corinth. This means we began with the "shut up" passages instead of beginning with women as co-equal, divine image-bearers in one-flesh intimacy with their male counterparts. Noted New Testament scholar David Scholer wrote, "The biblical text one chooses for one's starting point in the study of a doctrine or issue in Scripture becomes the lens through which one looks at all other texts."[2] Where you begin will determine where you conclude, and we began in the wrong place. Our trajectory was a dead end from the start.

What's more, we did not discern that the power struggle of domination and manipulation between the sexes was the result of sin. Domination and manipulation was not prescribed by the Lord God, it was merely a description of what the descent into self-worship did to the relationship between the sexes (Genesis 3:16). It did not describe the divine intention.

We remained ignorant of the horrendous bondage women were trapped in until the time of Jesus. Therefore we were generally unaware that Jesus redeemed women from the curse of sin, discipled women, and filled women with the Spirit.

Furthermore, we had taught that we no longer live in the time when the Spirit gifts the church with spiritual gifts. Therefore, all the references to women praying, prophesying, teaching, and working as apostles were considered totally irrelevant for women in today's church. We considered the era of Spirit-gifting a dispensation that had passed; that was then and now is now. We ignored the witness of women about how God's Spirit was gifting them to minister in today's church, except the limited role of ministering to women and children.

Our denominational tradition had read one side of the correspondence Paul sent to the church in Corinth and to Timothy at Ephesus, and we made eternal laws out of language in these occasional letters that was addressed to a specific disorder in these local churches. We seldom questioned the foolishness of making a law for the church for all time based on words for a specific occasion that we did not fully comprehend. We had ignored the genre, form, and content of the letters and read them as if they were a legal code. As free men and women in Christ, we found ourselves tied up by laws that we had created.

We placed Paul's occasional corrective letters above the biblical doctrine of the creation of women and Jesus' liberation of women.

We were oblivious to the biblical witness of the creation and liberation of women because we had not begun our study of women where the Bible begins the story of women.

Using the same scheme of biblical interpretation as our slaveholding forefathers had used in the 19th century to defend slavery, we silenced women with the words "women must not speak in the churches." Similarly, the slaveholders quoted the verse, "Slaves, be obedient to your masters." Both commandments were lifted out of occasional letters in ancient cultural and political contexts, and were separated from the redemptive storyline that runs throughout Scripture, from the creation of male and female to the liberating work of Jesus.

We accessed Scripture's authority for today's church through New Testament commands, examples, and necessary inferences, thereby turning the Bible into a rule book and ignoring the liberating work of God and the redemptive movement in Scripture. For example, we argued that since there are no commands or examples of women being pastors in the New Testament, women cannot be pastors today. This manmade grid that we put on the New Testament was, of course, a failed interpretive rationale. This same grid had justified the slavery of African Americans in the 19th century and the division in the Church of Christ over a cappella music in the 20th century.

So we began to ask ourselves hard questions, and we prayed and begged for the Spirit to lead us and mature us in Christ.

Scripture – What is it?

As an attorney for more than 30 years, I have regularly used the Texas Family Code, a systematic statement of family law. The code outlines the law in every circumstance for every citizen of Texas. If we similarly think of Scripture as a legal code, then we must try to harmonize the conflicts within the code, including those surrounding the role of women. We must somehow harmonize the two passages in Paul's letters that say women should be silent and never teach men with the facts that the Lord God also gifted Deborah to lead Israel in the Old Testament, raised up Junia to be an apostle, empowered Priscilla to teach Apollos, and affirmed women praying and prophesying in the Corinthian assemblies. The effort to harmonize all this is impossible because the underlying premise of the Bible as a legal code is dead wrong.

If the current Texas Family Code had in it as many apparent contradictions regarding the role of women as does the Bible, the governor would call an emergency session of the Texas Legislature to get the code reworded so that the laws contained therein could be easily understood with all contradictions removed. That's the way legal codes work.

But what if that is not the way the Bible works because it is not a legal code? Does not the Bible say, "The written code kills; the Spirit gives life?"

What if the Bible is fundamentally the True Story of the world, told over 2,000 years about the mighty acts of God to redeem the world?

What if there is redemptive movement in Scripture that changed the behavior of the actors in the drama as the storyline moved through time? Was this not happening in Matthew 19:1-9, about 29 A.D., when Jesus said that Deuteronomy 24 was no longer the Word of God for the people of God because Jesus had come to establish the kingdom of God? Is it not also true that the Jewish food laws of Leviticus were the Word of God for the people of God for 1,500 years but Jesus declared their usefulness had ended? Is not the story moving through time as God acts in creation, at the Exodus and Sinai, and then in Jesus Christ and at Pentecost?

Paul in his letter to Corinth certainly moved away from a legal vision of the kingdom of God and resisted those who argued for a legal jus-tification for their actions by saying, "All is lawful, but not helpful. All is lawful, but I will not be under the authority of anything" (I Corinthians 6:12-13). In every case, Paul says the legal question is inadequate. We need to ask better questions. So in 1 Corinthians he helps the Corinthians ask instead: Is it helpful? Is it an act that will lead us into bondage? Is it consistent with our identity as Christ's body? Is it consis-tent with our identity as temples of the Holy Spirit? Does it advance the proclamation of the gospel? Is the Spirit leading us to do this?

We live in a time that not only rejects the legalism of the past but sometimes has little respect for Scripture as spiritual authority. There are many in the church today who don't care what Scripture says. They love Jesus, but Scripture is secondary at best. For them, spiritual author-ity resides in experience and intuition. Yet ignoring Scripture is not an option; asking the Spirit to help us interpret Scripture is a much better option. Repenting of our past failures to interpret Scripture so that we can better equip the entire church for ministry is a still better option.

Though we reject the interpretive grids of the past that led us into oppression, we do not reject Scripture in order to announce the libera-tion of women by Jesus the Lord. In fact it is Scripture's witness to us and the witness of the Spirit among us that has brought us to strong convictions regarding the liberation of women for ministry. Our convic-tions have changed not by ignoring Scripture but by listening to the

Spirit's witness and embracing the witness of the entire canon from Genesis 1 through Revelation 22.

WHY BOTHER?

Those who exalt experience above Scripture as our spiritual authority might ask, "Why worry about Scripture? Why not just go with science or culture or intuition?" Many are doing just that. My skeptical friends ask, "Why bother reading a book that says, "Let there be a dome in the midst of the waters and let it separate the waters from the waters" (Genesis 1:6)? The Bible's ancient pre-scientific cosmology discredits Scripture in their minds.

We read it because Jesus read it and quoted it as Scripture. It tells us who God is, who we are, and for what purpose we live. We do not read it as a book of contemporary science; it isn't. Science creates technology – a force without morals, purpose or values. Einstein said science cannot tell us what is valuable. That is not what science does. We need science to unpack the mysteries of creation, improve the quality of human life, and build stronger communities. But only a revelation of God's identity and purposes in the world, which in turn reveals our identity and mission to us, tells us what we must do with the technology that science creates. Christian faith gives science the moral guidance, values and purposes that direct its uses.

I contend that the Bible gives a truer and much fuller account of what is going on in the world than do politicians, scientists, psychologists, and journalists. This Great Story declares that the creator God has redeemed the world from its bondage to death and a great narrative is being played out all around us in which we now take part. Hebrews 11:9-12 goes so far as to say that we are completing now what they started. The story is indeed told in an ancient book, but the God of the story is not only our contemporary, he is our future.

INTERPETATION – A HIGH CALLING

Along the way we are harassed by those who say there is no need to interpret Scripture because the issue regarding women is "plain as day." They halt all discussion just by saying, "The Bible says it; I believe it; that settles it." Others hinder the discussion with appeals to social practice, pointing out that since women lead businesses, universities, and governments, they should surely lead churches, too. Still others make claims of personal intuition, saying, "I just feel led to pastoral leadership."[3] Many settle for such inadequate solutions, which are clearly vulnerable to being manipulated by one's interests.

The position I take is that all Scripture texts must be interpreted, and there is no rational or spiritual way to show the infallibility of any interpretation. The centurion stood at the Cross and declared Jesus was the Son of God; others there saw nothing but a messianic imposter dying on a cross. Both saw the same events but interpreted them differently. This is not to say that we cannot by faith know Christ and the power of his suffering and resurrection. We can and we do! It is to say that Scripture and history are subject to interpretation.

Some people claim to see things exactly as they are all the time. Given Paul's statement that "now we see in part, prophecy in part, and know in part," we cannot agree with any claims of 20/20 vision. So we have good reason to exercise humility. Paul also declared that "we see through a mirror darkly now." None of this suggests that we do not see; we do. We see enough to witness on behalf of the risen Christ, but we do not see well enough to claim perfect insight. Even the apostle Peter described Paul's writings as difficult to interpret.

Yet we do not hold a relativistic view that denies a moral and spiritual truth outside of ourselves. Our position is a critically realistic one: we acknowledge that truth exists outside us but also recognize we can never know it perfectly. Even after we have diligently prayed and interpreted the Scripture faithfully in the Spirit, we will see only partially, so disagreement is inevitable. If we believe we are infallible on these matters, it stands that we would consider those who disagree with us to be ignorant, evil, or both. Whenever we claim infallibility, we dishonor the One who really is infallible.

What makes this so hard is what we have silently assumed about these issues yet never discussed with each other. We each come with preconceived understandings of Scripture, the role of women in the church, and the leading of the Spirit. Believing, for example, that we can easily harmonize all that Scripture says on the role of women reveals assumptions about the nature of Scripture and our own ability to know truth. Let's just admit that all of us come to this daunting task with silent assumptions.

In his book *Why I Am a Catholic*, G.K. Chesterton said:

[The Roman Catholic Church] does not, in the conventional phrase, believe what the Bible says, for the simple reason that the Bible does not say anything ... you cannot put a book in a witness box and ask it what it really means. The Bible by itself cannot be a basis of agreement when it is a cause of disagreement; it cannot be the common ground of Christians when one takes it allegorically and some literally.[4]

Chesterton is saying there must be an authoritative interpreter of Scripture and the church must embrace that calling. Scripture speaks infallibly when it is rightly divided. We seek to hear the once-for-all, historical, and biblical witness to the Word become flesh and the description of the new life in Christ. We are called to translate this into today's world.

As his disciples living in this new world in Christ, we acknowledge the inspiration and authority of Scripture in the church. We also recognize that Scripture is an instrument of the Spirit. The fact that Scripture is inspired means we must interpret it. If we did not think it uniquely inspired and authoritative, we would not bother to interpret it. We interpret Scripture now to hear God today. His Scripture is infallible in that it leads us into a saving relationship with God every time, but it is infallible only when it is discerningly interpreted in the Spirit.

We need to acknowledge up front that there is some ambiguity, accommodation to culture, and diversity within Scripture.

First, the intersection of the historical particularity of the past with the eternal Word leaves more ambiguity in Scripture than we might have expected. What do we do with holy wars, holy kisses, wearing veils, speaking in tongues, modes of baptism, and so on? What is the eternal Word in our historical particular? Sometimes it is not entirely clear. Like it or not, Scripture is a sprawling story told over thousands of years by numerous authors. Therefore our calling to interpret the ambiguities within this magnificent revelation of God in the world requires plenty of humility and diligence from us.

Secondly, the Lord God accommodated cultures in order to communicate to them in their own language and setting (1 Corinthians 9:19-25). For example, Paul told the Corinthian women to wear their hair up on their heads because that is what respectable women did in that culture. That was an accommodation to that culture. What is the eternal Word within texts where such accommodation to culture is apparent?

Thirdly, there is diversity within the essential unity in Scripture. The Deuteronomy law code and the Sermon on the Mount differ at significant points yet are united by a common relationship with the Lord God of Israel and Jesus. The differences are explained by the redemptive movement effected by the coming of Jesus to this world. This is not an insoluble problem. It is part of the nature of Scripture's revelation of God's will unfolding redemptively over time. The New Testament deals with this on every page as Paul and Jesus declare that what was the will of God under the law is no longer the will of God in these end times.

There are diverse witnesses inside a still greater unity. John's Gospel gives a witness to Jesus unlike Matthew's Gospel, yet they thunder in overwhelming unison their confession of Jesus as Savior and Lord of the world. Paul's counsel to women in 1 Corinthians 7 changes in his first letter to Timothy in Ephesus, written twelve years later. We seek to hear the Word of the Lord in these two letters written at different times to different circumstances.

Some act like the New Testament was written to the church 2,000 years ago but not to us. They argue we should now simply follow our culturally mandated intuitions. Others act as if the New Testament was written to us and not to the early church. They read Scripture like it is an email that God sent to us this morning!

We reject both alternatives as we acknowledge two inescapable realities: a 2,000-year separation from the time the ancient Scripture was written represents a huge historical and cultural distance, and we have to figure out our own place in the story told by that ancient Scripture. This means interpreting the ancient texts in their historical and cultural contexts and then teaching the same theology in a very dissimilar culture. Faithful interpretation and teaching in today's church will faithfully translate the ancient texts into our culture.

To be able to interpret and teach these Scriptures, we ask at least three questions: What did these texts originally mean to their readers? What do these texts mean for us in our culture? What must we do now in response to these messages? This is our task as disciples.

We also recognize that we come to Scripture from within a tradition – places from where the faith has been handed down. Today, we also interpret from within a wider postmodern culture that has renounced patriarchy and has adopted an egalitarian position both socially and legally.

2

Our Relationship to God and Scripture

As we listen to God speak through his ancient word to our culture, we discern through his Spirit and in the context of our faith community a pattern of how to live in our world. 1 Corinthians 2:13-16 says Christ's followers, while not infallible, must be alive in the Spirit in order to hear God and submit. If we are not operating in the Spirit, we will not receive the eternal Word. Apart from the Spirit's life in us, revelation will not happen.

THE UNITY THE SPIRIT GIVES

Apart from the Spirit, we will not read Scripture together in unity. But with the leading of the Spirit, we will sit together to hear God. We will not destroy the work of God because we simply ran out of patience, kindness, and humility (Romans 14 and Ephesians 4:1-3).

HEARING THE GOD OF SCRIPTURE

Our relationship with the Bible is transformed into a relationship with the God of the Bible who communicates to us through the Bible. We frame the authority of the Bible and our submission to it in terms of love, trust, and conversation with God. It is a movement from paper to person. It is not just an authority model but a relational model as well.[5] God is distinguishable from the Bible, having existed long before there was a Bible. Our relationship with the Bible's communication to us is to listen and love the one communicating to us. Words matter because they represent persons. We learn to listen, pay attention, absorb, and act on this communication. All of our listening is missional. If the Bible has caused us to love God and our neighbor, it has succeeded (2 Timothy 3:17).

ALWAYS BOTH WORD AND SPIRIT

Prayerful people may claim Jesus is just a mystic, a good man, a holy man, a Jewish rabbi, and a prophet – and all of them would claim God told them this is true. They claim authority to invent an alternative Christ with an alternative ethic, and they claim God's blessing on their revisions. But in every instance they ignore the eternal Word of God, who is the risen Jesus and his new covenant scriptures.

Spirit without Word also ignores what Scripture says about women in the interest of liberating women, relying solely on prayer and intuition, and separated from the historical revelation of God in Christ and the witness of Scripture. What may feel like freedom for women tears apart the inseparable Word *and* Spirit.

Word without Spirit ignores the current work of the Spirit in the lives and witness of women. The Word-only group pays no attention to the gifting of women by the Spirit to do the work of God in today's church.

A balance of Spirit and Word understands that Jesus the eternal Word pours out his Spirit to teach the church. The eternal Word authorized apostles and prophets to speak and write his words. The word is the sword of the Spirit. The Spirit works through the Spirit-filled church today and through her ancient Scriptures to teach and guide the church in diverse cultures everywhere. Word, Scripture, and the Spirit work together to guide and teach today's church.

STORY AND COMMANDMENT

Scripture is a grand meta-narrative, a covenant love story inside an enduring friendship. Scripture brings together Genesis 1:1, "In the beginning God created," with the end of all things in Revelation 22, "I make all things new."

Scripture tells us an identity-forming story, wooing us to the heart of God. When we are "all in," the story tells us what we must do.

Deuteronomy 6 says, "I am the Lord your God who called you out of Egypt, therefore you shall have no other gods before me..." Knowing the God of the story and our place in the story tells us what we must do. This was true in Exodus 19-20 and Matthew 5-7. Story and commandment are inseparable within Scripture.

CHARACTER AND COMMUNITY

Biblical interpretation is more about being good than being smart. We cannot interpret Scripture without first developing the virtues necessary to find the truth. The diligence, humility, and longsuffering it takes to discover, disagree, communicate, and embody the truth supports the search for truth in a diverse community. The truth is lived and discovered in a community where the Spirit sheds new light. The prophets are subject to the prophets in community (1 Corinthians 14).

We must not be naïve about ourselves. We do not approach any Scripture text as innocent children. A husband, for example, may have a dominant attitude toward people in general. By nature he leads, dominates, and is inflexible. He may then come to a biblical text on family leadership, reads it through his domineering glasses, and concludes he has a biblical mandate to boss, push around, and coerce his wife, even to the point of commanding her love.[6] If one's prejudice is so deep-seated that one reaches a conclusion before the evidence is considered, then prejudice renders impossible the accurate understanding of the text.

Do we possess the virtues necessary to grapple with the ambiguity and the diversity of Scripture's witness? How can there be an ethical or faithful use of Scripture unless we are a community capable of following the admonition to put "away falsehood, let everyone speak the truth with his neighbor, for we are members one of another" (Ephesians 4:25-32). Only a community of love and diligence after the truth can determine the proper use of Scripture in the life of the church. We will be blessed by hearing our brothers and sisters speak the truth in love as they see it. We will then learn to live in "humility and gentleness, patiently bearing with one another in love" (Ephesians 4:2). These virtues serve the truth, challenging us to consider other points of view within a community where belonging and identity do not depend on everyone agreeing with us.

AUTHORITY AND FREEDOM

Because Jesus is Lord, he is in charge, and we are free only as we are enslaved by him for his sake. So we possess Christ's freedom and his authority, not our own. Apart from Jesus, we are hopelessly enslaved to our own whims. So as we interpret Scripture, we bind ourselves to Jesus to live in covenant faithfulness to his mission as we struggle to "handle aright the word of truth." His absolute authority and our freedom in bondage to him deliver us from almost certain disaster as we read and interpret Scripture.

None of our interpretations on disputable matters must be allowed to destroy the work of God in the church (Romans 14-15). We have no reason to withdraw fellowship over these issues or to stop communicating with those with whom we disagree. The tension between authority and freedom holds us in responsible relationship with each other as we speak, discuss, and debate the truth in the love and the unity he gives.

KNOWLEDGE AND OBEDIENCE

The revelation of God through Christ leads to personal knowledge of God, and this personal knowing imparts to us eternal life. We are filled with the life of the age to come, which means we adore and obey God. Bodily obedience is a fruit of knowing God. We are always walking out our knowledge of God and our interpretations of Scripture. This testifies to the world that Jesus is "the Way, the Truth and the Life." We respect the Bible now in large part because of Spirit-filled, obedient witnesses. When Paul says, "You know those from whom you learned it" (2 Timothy 3:1, 4:15), he was suggesting that Timothy had read the lives of those who taught him even as he heard their verbal witness to Jesus, and that those obedient lives possessed compelling authority.

The way we do church, and more specifically the way we treat women in the church, testifies to who God is, who we are, and what God is doing in the world. Obedience flows out of relational knowledge of God.

UNITY WITHIN THE ARGUMENT

Let's look at what Bible-believing, evangelical disciples of Jesus have in common regarding Scripture. We believe that God has inspired Scripture and that God speaks through Scripture. So the issue is not the inspiration of the Bible. We believe authority is external to us. The external authority lies in an authoritative Person, a sacred book, the witness of the Spirit, and the living tradition of the church handed down by an authoritative community. This is the way God authoritatively mediates his will to us. We believe that our vision was distorted by the fall and that we cannot come to know God by reason or experience. God must reveal himself to us if he is to be known at all. We further believe that God has revealed himself by a Person's deeds and through a book that both reports and interprets those deeds. We believe he has given us the Spirit to illuminate spiritual reality in our minds and to guide us into all truth.

Other forms of authority – tradition, reason, and experience – may confirm the truths in Scripture, but they must submit to the witness of Jesus the eternal Word and the apostolic witness to him as written down by his apostles and interpreted by a community in the Spirit.[7]

Furthermore, we believe that we are not justified by believing rightly on the issue of women but by the faithfulness of God in Jesus Christ our Lord and Savior. We claim a unity of the Spirit that is centered in the confession of Jesus Christ the Lord.

Even knowing that our unity transcends the issue of women, it is never easy to care deeply for the brother or sister with whom we disagree and at the same time hold faithfully to the truth as we understand it. It can easily throw us into such cognitive dissonance that we either let go of the truth we have embraced or let go of an obligation for relationship with a disagreeing (and possibly disagreeable) brother or sister in Christ. It is a strange but hopeful reality that we most often grow and develop spiritually as we live within the tensions of the Christian life.[8]

3

An Imperfect Interpretation of the Entire Canon

It's wise to remember that no one has perfectly explained all the texts in Scripture, so we admit the position we take is not the only one. We look to see what makes the most sense of the texts and what reasons we have for believing A rather than Z. If those reasons are not warranted, we suspend belief. But we already have a conviction regarding the Lord's will in this church at this time, so we ask whether there is a corresponding direction discernible in the texts. After a season of listening together, we conclude there is.

NOT A PERFECT INTERPRETATION

Our quest is not for the perfect theory, the perfect interpretation of Scripture, or the perfect theology – only the best available. The main thing in life is not to try to figure everything out but to rely on God to provide what we need to accomplish his will in every circumstance, including the best theology for the job, and then to get on with that work.[9]

It disturbs us to admit that we are picking and choosing. Yet all of us pick and choose the Scriptures we consider important for today's church. The question is do we pick and choose in a way that honors God and embraces the Bible as God's Word for all time? To have an accurate reading of individual texts about women, we need to scope out the bigger story that Scripture tells.

INTERPRETIVE CENTER FOR THE CHURCH

I view all of Scripture through the lens of the story's hero, Jesus Christ, who constitutes the defining redemptive act of the story. I see this story as one of "liberation with a price" from beginning to end. The Great Drama of Scripture unfolds as follows:

Act 1: God creates – Genesis 1-2.

Act 2: Trouble ensues – Genesis 3-11.

Act 3: Israel is called – Genesis 12.

Act 4: Jesus redeems and is the one through whom God will ultimately consummate all of his creation in a new creation – The Four Gospels.

Act 5: The Spirit creates the end-times church – Acts 1-2.

Act 6: The Lord returns to resurrect the dead, properly judge the world, and create anew the entire planet – the Book of Revelation.

The end-times church is now in Act 5, and we are moving toward the coming of the Lord. The previous acts of the play and the coming sixth act of the play make sense of the story we find ourselves in today. Living in the fifth act, we find ourselves in an unfinished story, awaiting the Lord's coming. Reading the first four acts tells us what God is doing now. Genesis 1 and 2 is the very telling first act of the play. Jesus saw the first act as revealing the Lord's will to us and said it still contains the word of God for us today in a way the law of Moses does not (Matthew 19:1-9).

We tell all six acts of the Great Story today to mobilize the church for her mission, to clarify her identity, and call her to claim the story as her own. The story the Bible tells and the story we find ourselves in begins in Genesis 1 and ends with Revelation 22. Surprisingly enough, the imagery of Genesis 1 and 2 appears again in the visions of Revelation 21 and 22. But more importantly the dilemma of Genesis 3 is resolved in Revelation 21 and 22. This sprawling story has a theater, director, script, plot, actors, and one storyline. It is a grand meta-narrative, a "covenant love story inside an enduring friendship."

This is my model for understanding Scripture, and more particularly, for understanding the place of women in the church. This model for understanding gender includes the creation of the world by the God of love; the fall-separation; the place of Israel and the law in God's redemptive scheme; the ministry of Jesus Christ on this earth and his redemptive work as Savior and Lord of the world; the nature of the church and her ministry, the work of the Holy Spirit, and the mission of God in the world in the end times; and the coming new creation of the entire cosmos.

WOMEN IN THE TRUE STORY

Scripture sets the stage for our understanding in Act 1 by stating women are created as divine image-bearers: "So God created man in his image; in the image of God he created him; male and female he created them" (Genesis 1:27). Male and female live in co-equal, one-flesh intimacy. Furthermore, female is not a slave to man nor is she the property of man; she is his sustainer. Genesis 2 describes woman as man's "helpmeet," a term used of God seventeen times in Old Testament Scripture. It is not descriptive of inferiority but of partnership.[10] Psalms 40:17 refers to God as "my help (*ezer*) and my deliverer." The word *ezer* is translated in Scripture as "deliverer," "strength," and "power." Male and female together make humankind. Women are not misbegotten males, as Aristotle believed.

As a result of Act 2, the rebellion described in Genesis 3-11, men subjugated women and women sought to manipulate men. Instead of the mutuality and intimacy between two divine image-bearers, women are given an inferior status to men. Men and women are now in a power struggle of domination and manipulation. "Your desire shall be for your husband and he shall rule over you" (Genesis 3:16). The Hebrew meaning suggests the woman desires to "rule" her husband. So the desire is not for sex but for power. The Hebrew word also suggests the woman turns to her husband and away from the Lord. This passage predicts and describes the fallen desire in men and women to manipulate and dominate one another. It is not a prescription for how anyone should behave. We must get the story right here! The domination and manipulation of the sexes is not the divine intention. It is a fruit of the rebellion-fall-descent described not in creation, but in the fall.

Act 3, God's call of Israel to be a blessing to the nations, began the long road out of bondage to freedom. Yet the law could not make this right. The law of Moses improved woman's lot yet still accommodated the hardness of men's hearts (Deuteronomy 24:1-4 and Matthew 19:1-9). By the time of Jesus, women were valued pieces of male property, not quite considered fully human under the law. They live with better conditions than the Babylonians but are not treated as restored or redeemed to the divine intention (Deuteronomy 22-24).

Yet there are signs of redemption at work. Moses' sister Miriam leads all of Israel in worshiping the Lord who delivers (Exodus 15:1-18). Deborah, a prophetess and judge gifted by the Holy Spirit, appears in the narrative without precedence (Judges 4). According to the text, Deborah is a judge because the Lord has gifted her and raised her up to be judge. The prophetess Huldah spoke for God to the king of Israel (2 Kings 22). We move through Israel's history from the Old Testament prophetesses to the outpouring of the Spirit on all who call on the name of the Lord, thereby gifting men and women with the gift of prophecy (Acts 2:14-42).

WOMEN IN JESUS' TIME

During the period of Second Temple Judaism, from 586 B.C. to the fall of Jerusalem in 70 A.D., Jewish women typically were not supposed to study Scripture. One rabbi said it was better to burn the Torah than to give it to a woman to read. Some of the rabbis thanked God every day they were not Gentiles, a slave, or a woman. Women were ignored when the rabbis calculated numbers needed for a quorum in the synagogue. Women, Gentiles, and slaves did not count when forming the people of God. It was shameful for a rabbi to speak to a woman in public. Rabbis never discipled women. A rabbinic saying summed up the common attitude: "At the birth of a boy all are joyful, but at the birth of a girl all are sad."[11]

In Jesus' day and back through the history of Israel to David and before, polygamy was permissible for men but not for women, and divorce laws allowed men but not women to easily divorce their spouses. In the Roman world, women were considered inferior to men. Female infanticide was common. Most Roman households had one girl at most because of the common practice of killing a second female child. Men outnumbered women in the Empire.

ACT 4 – WOMEN'S REDEEMER

By contrast, Jesus disciples women in Act 4, something no other rabbi or Greek philosopher ever did. Luke 8 names women who followed Jesus. This is remarkable and unprecedented. In Luke 10:38-42, Jesus affirms Mary, who is sitting at his feet and being discipled. This is not a passage that disparages homemaking; the choice is not be a disciple or a homemaker. The passage is about the liberation of women from the power of sin, separation, and subjugation, the systematic devaluing and ignoring of women. Women are being called out of this world to follow Jesus, as are men. They will be part of the church as Spirit-filled members of the body of Christ on earth.

This begins a trajectory away from the rabbinical discipling of only men and the synagogue's formation solely around men. The significance of this is impossible to exaggerate. Jesus is calling all of us, male and female, to himself. We do not first become a homemaker or a businesswoman. We first follow Jesus, and then we follow the Spirit's leading to do the works God has called us to do.

PENTECOST INAUGURATES ACT 5

It appears that women were in the Upper Room and were included among those on whom the Spirit fell in Acts 1-2. Everyone present began speaking in other tongues as the Spirit enabled them. When the Spirit fell, the huge disturbance caused the crowd to accuse the speakers of drunkenness. In his sermon Peter defends what is happening and proclaims Jesus as Israel's Savior and Lord. Within the sermon is a reference to Joel 2, which contains the phrase "your sons and your daughters shall prophesy." Peter quotes this part of the passage. He appears to be defending women preaching as the fulfillment of prophecy. His argument is that in the end times, women and men will be gifted with the Spirit without regard to gender, based solely on "calling on the name of the Lord." Women are restored to their status with their male counterparts as children of God and complementary divine image-bearers.

The quote from Joel 2:28-32 continues with, "Yes, and on my menservants and my maidservants in these days I will pour out my Spirit and they shall prophesy." Not only will the sons and daughters of the house prophesy but the menservants and maidservants will step out of their places in the social order and join in prophesying. The end-times place of women is right in the middle of the body of Christ, using their gifts and talents for the glory of God as they are gifted by the Holy Spirit so to do. Any male disrespect or patronization is simply not appropriate at this moment in the story. The Lord Jesus has created a new community of fully empowered men and women through the power and presence of the Spirit of God. It happened on Pentecost Sunday, the harvest Sunday for Israel.

In summary, Jesus forever changed the place of women in the kingdom of God by:

1. Announcing the kingdom of God to women and men.
2. Discipling women and men.
3. Liberating women and men from the curse of the fall.
4. Giving the Spirit to women and men, including the gift of public prophesying.
5. Reconciling men and women together into one body.

This is liberation without precedent. Jesus is the unique liberator of humankind from the power of separation in the world. Sin had separated us, we sought to dominate and manipulate, we lost mutuality, and we became strangers. Jesus came to liberate all of us from this bondage. The reconciliation effected by Jesus Christ, the creator-redeemer, ends the sex wars and restores the dignity of male and female as envisioned in Genesis 1. Paul announces the achievement of Jesus Christ the Lord when he declares in Galatians 3:28, that "in Christ there is neither male nor female; all are one."

So we began with a good creation, two divine image-bearers who were equal before the Lord and each called to represent the Lord to his creation, and we end with a new creation accomplished by Jesus who came to redeem, reconcile, and restore. It is apparent that Jesus came to recover what was originally there but had been lost. The "re-" prefix before redeem, restore, and reconcile points to a prior relationship being recovered. The oneness of Genesis 1 is restored in Galatians 3:28 and the one who recovers it is Jesus. This is the redemptive movement of Scripture at play. We are to embody this redemptive movement on the earth and in the church.

MINISTRY IN THE FIFTH ACT

The framework for any biblical interpretation is the story Scripture tells of the mission of God and the formation of a community sent to participate in it. This is what the entire story is about. The mission of God is the framework, the clue, and the interpretive key for biblical interpretation. The aim of biblical interpretation is to fulfill the equipping purpose of the biblical writings.

Within the Old Covenant Scriptures the only ministry that was exclusively male was the priesthood. However, because Jesus abolished the Levitical priesthood and made every one of us a priest, there are clearly women priests (1 Peter 2:9). I see the resolution of women in ministry as connected to the wider issue of mobilizing the entire church for ministry. Ministry is not a calling for a few males who go to seminary; it is calling the entire church to participate in full-time ministry (Ephesians 4:1-3).

We have defined ministry as a few official activities that only men do, so ministry became a professional men's club. The problem with our discussion of ministry is not so much in the answers as in the question. The transformation that Paul's vision calls for would not be to let a few more specifically gifted women share with a few men the rare roles of domination; it would be to reorient the notion of ministry so that there would be no one ungifted, no one not called, no one not empowered, and no one dominated.[12] Only that would live up to Paul's call to "lead a life worthy of our calling."

Within Paul's charismatic vision of ministry in 1 Corinthians 12-14 there is not one ministerial role that we could argue is gender-specific. There are as many ministerial roles as there are members of the body of Christ, and that means that more than half of them belong to women. There are no male or female gifts of the Spirit.

Paul in 1 Corinthians 14 is telling the prophets, both male and female, to be mutually submitted to one another. Clearly women are included as prophets who are to be subject to the prophets, whether male or female. Female prophets were accorded no less authority in 1 Corinthians 11 and 14 than were male prophets. Gender was not an issue. Paul also told the entire Ephesian church to "be submitted to one another out of reverence for Christ." As a pastor-leader, I am submitted to my brothers and sisters in Christ. The notion that men do not need to submit to everybody else in Christ has no foundation in Scripture. I receive guidance, encouragement, and rebuke from men and women all the time, and none are violating Scripture.

It is also crystal clear that all those who have become children of God through the redeeming work of Jesus Christ have been ordained and authorized to serve. Otherwise Paul would not be admonishing the entire Ephesian church to "live a life worthy of the calling" and he would not refer to the entire church being equipped for "the work of ministry" (Ephesians 4:1-3). Ministry is not a special word describing what a few ordinands do; it is a common word to describe what the entire baptized, and therefore ordained, church does.

As the Puritan preacher John Robinson commented while watching a shipload of his pilgrim brothers and sisters sail off from England for Massachusetts, "The Lord hath yet more light and truth to break forth from his holy word." Paul's vision of every member being empowered is one fragment of the gospel vision that has yet to find its reformation. When we create certain exclusive ministry systems run by a few professional males, we are acting more like Old Covenant Israel than the New Covenant church.

THE STORY AND TODAY'S CHURCH

We find ourselves as disciples of Jesus Christ in an incomplete story. We are part of this ongoing story of the people of God, called to be his witnesses "until he comes." All who receive the Spirit live the life of the future together until all things are restored by Jesus at his coming. We live in hope regarding who and what is coming when the Lord Jesus Christ will complete, perfect, and transform all things. Until then we see in part, prophesy in part, know in part, and see through a mirror darkly. Yet though we see imperfectly and only in part, we do see. As we come to see more clearly, we are called to live more closely to the divine intention. The journey will never end.

Because we have not arrived, and neither had the New Testament era church, the question is more about the trajectory than it is the practice of the early church. The question is more about what God is doing than a corrective text written to one local church.

The plot of the Bible, the story of the Bible, and the behavior of women in that plot and story reveal to me an increasing expansion of women in church ministries. We sometimes misread the Scriptures, fall back into power-grabbing sin and temporarily stop the inevitable move of God, and quench him for a season and in some places, but ultimately we will not defeat what God is doing in the world. His Word will be lived out in this world.

We contend that it is God's will that all of the church, both women and men, be liberated and encouraged to fulfill the mission as each are gifted and called. This is not an act of interpretive chaos; it is the declaration that everyone in the church is free to do all of God's good.

I am certainly aware of the verses in 1 Corinthians 14 and 1 Timothy 2 that call for women in those churches at that time to be silent. However, I am reading these passages in the light of the redemptive movement in Scripture and the place of men and women in the True Story of the world. So let's now talk about biblical interpretation and how we understand the tensions within Scripture as to the role of women in the church and ministry.

4

The Interpretive Circle – Normative, Descriptive, and Corrective Texts

Given the obvious diversity of texts in Scripture, we seek to properly interpret them as they appear within the redemptive storyline of Scripture. One way to discern the meaning of these texts is to understand them as normative, descriptive, or corrective. We function in an interpretive circle regarding Scripture, moving back and forth between what we assume to be normative and descriptive texts and what we assume are corrective texts, and seeing how well the data is explained by this relationship. We are always refining, learning anew, and revising our convictions.[13] We never stop listening to those who disagree with us. Let me explain what I mean by normative, descriptive, and corrective texts.

Normative texts embody the controlling vision of the True Story, including women within that vision (Genesis 1:26-28 and 2:18-25, Luke 8:1-3 and 10:38-42, Matthew 19:1-9, Acts 2:14-36, Galatians 3:28). These texts reveal male and female as co-equal divine image-bearers, created for one-flesh intimacy by the Lord God. These texts also reveal that Jesus discipled women and redeemed women from the curse of the fall. Furthermore, these texts describe the outpouring of the Spirit on all women who call on the name of the Lord. At Pentecost, women are receiving the Spirit along with the men present, including the gifts of the Spirit. The conclusion is that men and women are one in Christ. Sin's destruction of that oneness has been recreated in the new creation Christ brings. Given the dignity of women in the creation and the recovery of her dignity in Christ's redemption, the question becomes, "By what authority would Christ's church, his body on earth, restrain women from doing whatever the Spirit of God has raised them up to do?"

WOMEN IN THE EARLY CHURCH

Descriptive texts describe the church's embodiment of God's redemptive action in Jesus Christ. Do we see the normative vision of women in Scripture beginning to be embodied? The answer is yes. Paul describes women praying and prophesying in the assembly (1 Corinthians 1l:2-16, 12-14). While living in Corinth, Paul stayed with Aquila and Priscilla, a married couple who worked with Paul and who risked their lives for his sake (Romans 16:3-4). Priscilla and Aquila taught Apollos, a well-known preacher from Alexandria (Acts 18:24-26). The fact that her name often appears first likely means she was the most dynamic teacher of the two. In any case Paul does not hesitate to name women as exercising leadership in the early church. Luke and Paul recorded this for the church to read and ponder.

In his letters, Paul greets women who were significant in the various churches: Apphia and two other leaders in Colossae (Philemon), Nympha in Laodicea (Colossians 4), and Euodia and Synctyche (Philippians 4). In Romans 16:1, Paul encourages the recipients of the letter to greet Phoebe, whom he calls a deacon. The word translated "servant" is also used to describe Paul, Timothy, Tychichus, Apollos, Epaphras, and Christ himself. So if this was an office for these men, it was an office for this woman.

He also refers to Phoebe who brings the letter to Rome as a *prostatis*, a benefactor that is referred to in other places as "those over you in the Lord" (1 Thessalonians 5:12) or to designate church officials who preside over a congregation (1 Timothy 3:4-5, 5:17). Paul encourages the Roman church to welcome Phoebe and to provide whatever she needs. In Romans 16:7, Paul sends greetings to a missionary couple, Andronicus and Junia, whom he calls "prominent among the apostles." Apostle means "one sent with authority." There is no doubt that the Greek translated Junia as feminine and that Paul is referring to a woman apostle.

From the Book of Acts we know that Greek women of high standing were attracted to Paul's preaching (Acts 16:14, 17:4). Such women would not be attracted to a movement that did not treat them as equals. Their little corner of the Roman Empire treated women with greater deference than any other. The church in Philippi met in the house of Lydia, a seller of purple. The fact that Paul visited her on his way out of town indicated she was the leader of the church. If the church met in your house, you were the church's leader (Acts 16:35-40).

CORRECTIVE TEXTS

The corrective texts regarding women appear in two letters, 1 Corinthians 14:34-35 and 1 Timothy 2:8-15. It is important for us to faithfully interpret these letters and to place their content within the wider circle of revelation.

One rule of interpretation is that we bring the clear things that already appear in many places in Scripture to bear on the obscure or difficult texts. When discussing a corrective text, Paul is addressing particular problems. The themes he discusses, the points he emphasizes, and the way he constructs the arguments are determined by the nature of the problem he is addressing. The corrective texts do not tell us what women are doing in the church or what Paul envisioned women doing in the churches; they only correct abuses.

Because we acknowledge that these letters from first-century apostles have authority over us, we want to hear the eternal Word in the historical particulars of these letters. We believe we are called to study and handle very carefully these ancient texts through which God will move on us (2 Timothy 3:16-17). We seek to hear God in our time.

But if we are to understand what God said, we will need to understand something of how he said it. The fifteen letters of Paul are written to specific churches at specific times and places. In every letter except the Ephesian letter, Paul is addressing specific issues in specific local churches. He is not writing these letters to every church; he is writing each letter to one church. If we take the literary type seriously, we know there will probably be words spoken to churches that are written for our edification and righteousness but are not commands for us today. Clearly a corrective passage in a letter such as Corinthians or Timothy corrects abuses in Corinth and in Ephesus. They do not correct the rest of the New Testament.

If we wrongly assume that these corrective passages are intended to correct the rest of the New Testament, we are disregarding the letter for what it is: an occasional document addressed to a specific church issue. Whatever eternal Word exists in these historical particulars will have to be discerned through prayer and reflection on the whole of Scripture and the work of Jesus Christ as creator and redeemer.

What does it mean to faithfully interpret letters in Scripture? None of us believe it means to regard every verse on the same level, or as permanently and literally applicable to all Christians in all circumstances. Within the New Testament we seemed to have found no difficulty in setting aside the literal observance of women covering their hair (1 Corinthians 11:2-16), the rules for the care of widows (1 Timothy 5), the holy kiss, and on and on. So how did we arrive at these practices and what should our way of applying these texts be?[14]

Paul tells Timothy to take a little wine for his stomach and to bring his cloak. We believe these are occasional words, no longer important for us. However, we do believe Paul's declarations of who Christ is and his call to a holy life to be eternal words for the church (1 Timothy 4:1-5). The challenge comes in knowing the difference between occasional words and eternal words.

We believe that Scripture edifies the church and builds her up in the Lord, but we do not consider every admonition in these letters to be a command to today's church. For example, I was taught that the admonition in 1 Corinthians 16:2 to "put aside and take up whatever extra you can" was an eternal word for the church; a commandment mandating weekly collections for today's church. After a careful study of the text, I realized that verse was a one-time admonition to the Corinthian church to gather up her gifts for the Jerusalem church so that Paul might pick them up on his way to Jerusalem and disburse them to the famine-stricken church in Jerusalem. It was an urgent one-time request, not an eternal command for today's church. Paul in 2 Corinthians said that this collection for the church in Jerusalem was not a commandment of the Lord but a work of freedom in the Spirit (2 Corinthians 8, 9).

Treating this specific and temporary admonition as a norm for all time far exceeds the intent or authority of the text and obscures its real meaning. Yet such was our predilection to treat occasional counsel as laws for all time, when in fact the Corinthian letter itself warns us against making legal codes out of Scripture.

The fact that Paul's counsel to unmarried women in 1 Corinthians 7 differs from that in 1 Timothy 5 does not mean he is contradicting himself. It means he is talking to two different churches about marriage at different times and in different life situations. Yet if a preacher is going to preach on marriage in the end times, he should use both passages and ask the Spirit to expand our awareness of New Covenant teaching.

Recognizing the degree to which any scriptural counsel was conditioned by the conventions of the time should serve as a caution against trying to transfer such directives directly into the different conditions of today's church. In doing so, we do not deny the authority of that teaching. Rather we affirm the relevance of the teaching to the particular historical circumstances for which it was written.

Teaching on women and men loses much of its authority if it does not take into account the different circumstances of today's church. Clarity within the so-called "face value" of an ancient text is not always achievable and not always faithful to the divine intention for the church today.[15] However, we must still ask what the eternal Word is saying to us today in this ancient text. To answer that we must look at the underlying theological vision that gives all of these texts meaning, then and now.

5

New Creation and Culture

Paul says in 2 Corinthians 5:16-19 that all who are in Christ are a new creation. He has already declared in Galatians 3:28 that there is neither Jew nor Greek, bond nor free, male nor female. In our baptism into Christ and through the power of the Spirit we enter into the new order of the new creation where the old distinctions have been obliterated. What has been obliterated is the significance the empire attached to these fundamentally divisive distinctions through which it preserved status and order.

Paul's worldview, by contrast, is charged with the end-times vision of new creation. He sees all things through the framework of the new creation. Paul contends that on becoming one in Christ, one's significance is not found in preserving any of these old uncrossable boundaries.[16] The old ways of valuing and conferring significance based on gender, race, and social status are gone forever as "all are one in Christ."

We come to Paul's letters and the corrective passages with a strong awareness that we now live in a new world. The story is moving toward the recovery of oneness. The normative passages that reveal woman's place in the True Story of the world point to the redemption and recovery of women's dignity and created place (Genesis 1:27, 2:24, Matthew 19:1-9, Galatians 3:28). At the same time, the filling of all men and women with the Spirit dramatically mobilizes the entire church for mission. Women are teaching, prophesying, and ministering as apostles. Jesus Christ has liberated women to do his will and his work.

JESUS AND CULTURAL RELATIVITY

We must continually step back and acknowledge the person, works, and acts of Jesus to be of primary importance (1 Corinthians 15:1-9). Jesus the Lord is what Elton Trueblood called "the place to stand." Jesus and his gospel of the kingdom of God existed before Paul and stands over Paul as Jesus' apostle to the nations. What Jesus did and is now doing is far more important than any admonition Paul ever made. This was true regarding slavery and it is true regarding women.

Jesus, the eternal Word of God, transcends all cultures and all historical distance. Paul is announcing Jesus and interpreting Jesus to the nations. Paul's words are critically important as an inspired apostle of Jesus Christ, as he translates this gospel from Palestine to the nations of the world. Yet Jesus himself remains most important. Paul even declared he "knew nothing among them except Jesus and him crucified." Paul is announcing and pastoring the redemptive work of Jesus to the whole creation.

We will argue now that culture, then and now, plays a part in our interpretation of Scripture. We will also argue that knowing and acknowledging the literary type of a passage of Scripture – in this case, letters – helps us to interpret Scripture. Also, we will acknowledge an ambiguity and lack of clarity within certain verses, an accommodation to culture in other verses, and Paul's diverse counsel to different churches at different times in different circumstances. We contend that a great redemption is at work and that in Jesus, God has provided a unique revelation (Ephesians 1-3).

Though we realize that culture and literary type play a part in interpreting Scripture, we are not riding a wave of cultural relativity; rather we are translating the faith into our culture. We begin with the matters of the kingdom gospel, the matters Paul described as of first importance as set out in 1 Corinthians 15:1ff. We are aware that from the beginning there were also disputable matters (Romans 14, 15). This means Scripture is not swallowed up by cultural relativity but that all Scripture is interpreted within real ancient cultures and that we are called to translate these truths into our culture.

NEW CREATION AND 1 CORINTHIANS 11

What was the significance of the new creation for the male-female relationship? The new creation restored the essential elements of the first creation – namely the mutuality of the sexes and the differentiation of men from women (Genesis 1, 2).[17] In 1 Corinthians 11:3-16, Paul addresses the differentiation of the sexes – women behaving as women and men behaving as men in ways appropriate to their culture. This passage is not about subordination of women to men; it has to do with women wearing head coverings so they don't shame themselves within the Corinthian culture. Paul writes:

> I praise you for remembering me in everything and for holding to the traditions just as I passed them on to you. But I want you to realize that the head of every man is Christ, and the head of the woman is man, and the head of Christ is God. Every man who prays or prophesies with his head covered dishonors his head. But every woman who prays or prophesies with her head uncovered dishonors her head – it is the same as having her head shaved. For if a woman does not cover her head, she might as well have her hair cut off; but if it is a disgrace for a woman to have her hair cut off or her head shaved, then she should cover her head. A man ought not to cover his head since he is the image and glory of God but woman is the glory of man. For man did not come from woman but woman from man; neither was man created for woman but woman for man. It is for this reason that a woman ought to have authority over her own head, because of the angels. Nevertheless, in the Lord the woman is not independent of man, nor is man independent of woman. For as woman came from man, so also man is born of woman, but everything comes from God. Judge for yourselves: is it proper for a woman to pray to God with her head uncovered? Does not the very nature of things teach you that if a man has long hair, it is a disgrace to him, but that if a woman has long hair it is her glory? For long hair is given to her as a

covering. If anyone wants to be contentious about this we have no other practice – nor do the churches of God.

Paul is speaking into a hierarchical culture, but his concern is with the women in the Corinthian church whose shameful disrespect for cultural expectations is dishonoring their husbands. This overriding concern must be kept in mind as we read this difficult passage of Scripture.

Verses 8 and 9 in the passage reference the Genesis 2 account of creation, in which woman is created as man's *ezer*, or strong helper. In verse 10 Paul says, "For this reason the woman ought to have authority on her head." Where in Scripture did Paul find the idea that power or authority was placed on the head of a woman? In Genesis 2:18, where *ezer* often is translated "helpmate" but is best translated "strength or authority." That is the way it is most often translated in the Old Testament, where it refers to the Lord God as the *ezer*, or the strong helper. So Genesis 2:18 is best translated: "I will make the woman a power or strength corresponding to the man."[18]

Paul uses the word "head" in the literal sense, as that which ought to be covered, and also figuratively, for the authority figure in the ancient household. He clearly uses it in the figurative sense in verse 3 and in the literal sense in verses 4-6. The figurative sense can mean authority or source. Because he is quoting Genesis 2, which envisions woman as created from man, source is a viable translation of the word *kephale* as used in verse 3.[19]

Paul is not arguing for the subordination of women based on the order of creation. His argument is a series of three doublets – man-Christ, woman-man, and Christ-God – which make the point that a unity of will and purpose pervades all three. Man and woman are called to a unity of purpose similar to the other two relationships.[20] Remember Paul's singular purpose here is correcting the Corinthian church women's shameful disrespect for cultural expectations, which is in fact dishonoring their husbands.

Headship focuses on the unity of will and purpose between a man and a woman. The emphasis of chapters 11-14 is on conduct in relationships within the church. The problem centered on Gentile women and men in church who were either unaccustomed to or unsympathetic with traditions and customs. This was why Paul begins and ends this section with appeals to those traditions and customs. He argues that the Corinthians should honor local traditions regarding the way women dress in public and that this should become their custom.

Paul argues that a man dishonors his head by covering it in worship and that a woman dishonors hers by not covering it. He argues this mainly on the basis of nature as he observed it; that men everywhere have shorter hair while women have longer hair (verses 5-6, 13-15). His main point was that men should follow the dress and hair codes that indicate they are male and women should follow the dress and hair codes that indicate they are female. Paul was arguing that the existence of the male and female brought honor and praise to the other.

By creating man in his image, God had set his own glory in man. Man exists to God's praise and honor, and is to live in relationship to God so as to be his glory. Because woman was created for the glory of the man, her disregard of distinctions between the sexes brought shame on the man whose glory she was intended to be. Paul does not deny that woman was created in God's image or that she also was God's glory. His point was *singular*. She is related to man as his glory, a relationship that is jeopardized by her present actions. Paul envisions men and women as both the glory of another and therefore both have an obligation not to cause shame to their "heads." Since they are the glory of different persons, they must use different means to avoid shaming their heads."[21]

Woman was man's glory because she came from man and was created for him. She is not thereby subordinate to him but necessary for him. She exists to his honor as the one who having come from man is the one companion suitable to him, so that he might be complete and that together they might form humanity.[22] His point was that it did not happen the other way around. Genesis 2:18 described woman as a helper suitable for him, corresponding or appropriate to as an equal, in contrast to the animals. Woman was created because man needed her strength.

The bottom-line issue in this text has to do with "shame" (verses 4, 5, 6, 13, and 14) in a culture where shame counted for everything. Woman is described as man's glory, not his inferior (verses 7-9). In verse 10, Paul says "she ought to have authority over her head because of the angels." This may refer to angels present in the corporate gatherings who will be offended by the dishonoring of the husbands.

Paul then says, "Nevertheless, in the Lord woman is not independent of man, nor is man independent of woman. For as woman came from man, so also man is born of woman. But everything comes from God" (verses 11-12). He is qualifying here everything he has said regarding the issue of head coverings in the Corinthian culture in order to declare the mutual interdependence of women and men in the Lord. This declaration in the Lord, that both are in need of the other, and as woman comes from man so does man come from woman, seems clearly designed to keep the earlier argument from being read as subordination for the woman.[23] 1 Corinthians 7:1-2 also describes the authority of a woman over her husband's body and the authority of a married man over his wife's body.

So when the passage is read carefully, Paul is arguing for the differentiation of women within that culture. The created distinction between men and women should be honored in the church. Paul opposed symbolic gender-bending actions. He was also arguing for the mutual interdependence of men and women, not the subjugation of women to men in the Lord.

Clearly Paul placed no restriction on women from praying or prophesying in the assembly. He assumed this was happening and would continue. He simply asked that the women wear their hair properly for that culture. The passage deals with women who are praying or prophesying in an assembly where men and women are present. The scandal in the Corinthian culture was the women's disregard for the proper way to cover or wear their hair in meetings where men are present.

Paul was not addressing social issues that we are familiar with today. Visit another culture today and you will discover many societal assumptions, expectations, and constraints, some of which involve the way people dress and wear their hair. In a Western culture, a man would not go to a formal dinner party wearing a bathing suit nor would a woman attend a beach picnic wearing a wedding dress. In Paul's day, gender was marked by hair and clothing styles. We can tell from statues, vase paintings, and other period artwork how this worked out in practice. There was social pressure to maintain appropriate distinctions.

The only women in Corinth who wore their hair down in public were prostitutes. If an unbeliever looked in on a Christian assembly and saw women with no head covering and her hair down, it would have had the same effect on their reputation as it would if someone in contemporary Texas culture looked into a church and found the women all topless.

The women in Corinth had probably been taught, as had the Galatian churches, that in Christ there was neither male nor female. They knew that in the Messiah they were all equally welcome and equally valued as the renewed people of God. Perhaps some of the women took Paul's words to mean they were free from the normal social conventions and proceeded to remove their usual head covering and unbraid their hair. We do not know why they did it, but we do know they did it and that Paul opposed their behavior by insisting they maintain gender differentiation in their assemblies.

When reading this passage it is crucial to keep the underlying and singular point of this passage in mind at all times. In the Christian assemblies, it was important for both men and women to be their truly created selves, to honor God by being who they were, and to not blur the lines by pretending to be someone else. For Paul it was clear that when the new community gathers, we are anticipating the restoration of all creation (1 Corinthians 15:27-28).[24] God made humans male and female and gave them authority over the world (Genesis 1:26-28 and Psalms 8:4-8). And if humans are to reclaim their authority over the world, this will come about as they worship the true God, as they pray and prophesy in his name, and are renewed in his image by living out what they were made to be and celebrating the genders God has given them.

Paul did not criticize women who were exercising a leadership role. He was happy about their public praying and giving a prophetic message or discourse. But he was deeply unhappy about any assumptions that gender equality meant gender sameness or gender interchangeability, and even more unhappy about their indifference to the principle of respect and respectability. Most seriously of all is their indifference to whether a questionable dress code might distract others from attending to the things of God in public worship.[25]

We should certainly stress the equality of men and women but should be very careful about implying identity. This passage insists that both men and women need to be themselves rather than for one to try to become a clone of the other.

1 CORINTHIANS 14:34-35

Two chapters later in 14:34-35, Paul abruptly says, "Women should remain silent in the churches. They are not allowed to speak, but must be in submission, as the law says. If they want to inquire about something they should ask their husbands at home; for it is disgraceful for a woman to speak in the church."

As a free man, Paul has already put himself temporarily under the law for the sake of the gospel (9:19-25). He is certainly not interested in making a law where there was never one. He was asking the Corinthian women to also make a temporary accommodation to their culture for the sake of the gospel. He is asking women to do what he had already done. To ask their own husbands at home suggests they were offering questions in the presence of other men in the assembly, something considered disgraceful in that culture (verse 35).

That society expected only men to publicly ask questions. Additionally, the women usually had very little knowledge of Greek, the language spoken in the assembly and were typically ignorant of the Scripture. With few exceptions, neither the Jewish or non-Jewish women had been taught Scripture.[26]

Paul counseled the wives to exercise their freedom by asking their husbands at home (1 Corinthians 14:34-35). The fundamental admonition was for them to learn. Most Jewish rabbis did not think women could learn. Paul did, and he admonished husbands to help their wives rather than oppress them. Also this counsel for order in the assembly is given to married women, not to all women. Clearly it was directed at a specific issue in the church at Corinth.

The central concern was for order and decency (14:33). Notice the flow of the entire context. Male prophets are told, "Don't all talk at once. Be silent in the church." Male and female tongue speakers are told, "If there is no interpreter, be silent in the church." Married women with Christian husbands are told, "Don't ask questions during the assembly and don't chat. Ask your husbands at home and be silent in the church."

No matter how seriously you take the "women keep silent" passages, it is profoundly unbiblical to let those passages overcome the passages about "what women do."[27] In line with the prophecy from Joel cited in Acts 2:17 on the day of Pentecost, "Your sons and daughters shall prophecy," women in the Corinthian congregation were praying and prophesying in the assembly in 11:2-16. In 14:34-35 some women were speaking in an instructional setting. The common element in the two texts is not "women speaking in public" but women evidencing disrespect for decorum and propriety, thus contributing to chaos and disruption.

The women in chapter 11 were flouting commonly accepted cultural norms, with resultant disrespect to their husbands. The women in chapter 14 were impeding instruction by their disruptive, dishonoring, and incessant questioning. We know that Paul in chapter 14 is not contradicting what he said in I Corinthians 11, where he fully supported women praying and prophesy while urging them to honor the sexual differentiation of their culture.

Because 1 Corinthians 14:34-35 is an occasional counsel to handle disruptions that made effective preaching of the gospel impossible in that culture, it is highly unwise and oppressive of us to make Paul's words an eternal law for all churches for all time. Given the fact women were speaking in the assembly according to chapter 11, this passage was evidently written to correct disorder created by women without knowledge and with little concern for the edification of the church. One thing is clear: for the sake of the gospel, Paul accommodated the culture in both Corinthian passages.

However, we do not live in that culture anymore. In fact we live in a culture where such "shame" is incomprehensible and to accommodate it would discredit the church.[28] We must be faithful to the gospel and Paul's teaching while being aware of the different culture we live in today. Treating these directives in an occasional letter as eternal law for all time makes the corrections the norm for today's church in a way that far exceeds the intent or authority of the text, thereby obscuring its real meaning for that culture and ours.

Occasional letters should not be read as eternal laws, but as letters written to us indirectly as disciples of the same Jesus. Our task is to discern the Word of God in these ancient letters for us today. If Paul's occasional directive that "women must be silent" is interpreted as a law for all times and places in the churches, then this passage silences women in any assembly, including house church, Bible classes, or staff meetings. Clearly the passage, if an eternal law for the church, is violated scores of times every week in every church in the land!

After looking at 1 Corinthians 11:2-16 and 1 Corinthians 14, it is clear to me that a lot of ambiguity still exists in the text, even after 2,000 years of interpretation. In the Spirit and with a tremendous amount of background knowledge of the text, we still do not know what to make of Paul's reference to the angels. We are not even sure whether the text is talking about a veil on women's heads or the hair being up on the head. Neither are we certain of the import of Paul's words that women come from men but also that men come from women in the Lord. These words seem to turn in a different direction from the first part of this section.

Paul was clearly intent in chapter 14 on stopping the practice of married women asking questions within the assembly. He referred to this behavior as shameful. Other than that, we are not sure what behavior he was addressing. We have just one end of the correspondence.

None of this is to doubt Paul's inspiration or authority. It is to say that this is a letter written to specific behavioral issues at a specific time and place.

Part of our frustration is our desire for Paul to say more than he said. We are frustrated with Paul's pastoral letter and its failure to answer all of our questions. It does not occur to us that we need to humbly ask better questions, leaving the ambiguity to stand on its own. Do we really have to answer all of these questions to learn from the text? Should we expect Paul in a very conflicted pastoral circumstance as he goes from issue to issue to give us a fully developed view of women in the church? Apparently not.

6

1 Timothy 2:8-15 – Corrective or Normative Word?

I desire, then, that in every place the men should pray, lifting holy hands without anger or argument; also that the women should dress modestly and decently in suitable clothing, not with their hair braided, or with gold, pearls, or expensive clothes, but with good works, as is proper for women who profess reverence for God. A woman should learn in quietness and full submission. I do not permit a woman to teach or to assume authority over a man; she must be quiet. For Adam was formed first, then Eve. And Adam was not the one deceived; it was the woman who was deceived and became a sinner. But women will be saved through childbearing – if they continue in faith, love and holiness with propriety (1 Timothy 2:8-15).

The background of Paul's first letter to Timothy was a heresy of "unsound words" in the church in Ephesus. Paul described this heresy as "myths and endless genealogies. Such things promote controversial speculations rather than advance God's work which is by faith" (1:4). The dominating mythology of Ephesus was propagated to all its citizens by the Artemis religious fertility cult, which was housed in a massive temple. Acts 19:23-40 testifies to the powerful hold Artemis had on her Ephesian subjects. Selling Artemis images was big business and Paul's gospel announcement had damaged sales. This led to the riot described in Acts 19. It is very likely the mythologies supporting the worship of Artemis constituted the background to 1 Timothy.

Everything Paul said about the myths conformed perfectly to the Artemis mythology.[29]

The heresy propagated in the temple of Artemis offered not only a vastly different vision of God but of women as well. The temple was run by women who surrounded themselves with castrated male priests. Their worship included eliminating normal sexual relations; these women despised marriage, childbearing, and childrearing. It was theological heresy, and Paul insisted the women stop teaching this mythology that demeaned sex, disparaged males, and denied creation (1 Timothy 4:1-5).

The entire letter of 1 Timothy deals with the false teachers mentioned in 1:3ff and Timothy's role in quelling their influence. The men are admonished in 2:1-8 to pray for all people and to stay out of quarrels engendered by false teaching. The women are admonished in 2:9-15 to present and conduct themselves in a manner appropriate for godly women. Paul was effectively countering the immodest, sexually provocative, and extravagant dress birthed by the mythological vision of women (2:9-10).

Paul continued to address in 2:11-12 the problem of insubordination, moving from dress and demeanor to the realm of teaching.[30] He began by telling the women, who have no background in the Old Covenant Scriptures and whose religious convictions have been formed by the Artemis cult, to "learn in quietness in full submission. I do not permit a woman to teach or to assume authority over a man; she must be quiet" (2:11-12). He says this because the false teachers apparently taught that the Artemis mother-goddess created woman first. Paul is correcting this teaching with a reminder that in Genesis Adam was created first.

Based on woman's supposed priority in creation and their direct connection to their goddess Artemis, the false teachers also promoted the idea that women were morally superior to men. In the face of this claim Paul wanted to establish that Eve was susceptible to temptation, not because he wanted to demonstrate women's inferiority but to call into question the false teachers ideas of women's superiority.[31]

There are two views of 1 Timothy 2:11-12. One holds that this text forbids women from teaching or exercising authority over men because of the order of creation. Proponents of this view maintain the Genesis material in verses 13-14 provides the reason for the prohibition in verses11-12 and conclude that these sanctions are to be applied universally. The other view holds that this was a temporary restraint to curb the inordinate conduct of certain Ephesian women who were teaching the heresy mentioned in 1:3-7 as the reason for the epistle. In this view the Genesis material in verses 13-14 provides an example or explanation of the dire consequences of Eve's deception as a parallel to what is going on in Ephesus.

The contents of the letter and the context of chapters 1 and 2 strongly suggest the second option is the better interpretation and application. Just as verses 9-10 are to be understood in terms of ancient cultural values and are addressed to the threat of false teachers in Ephesus, so also are the admonitions to silence and submission in verses 11-12. In this view, verses 11-12 are a temporary stipulation intended for the particular situation in Ephesus and not as universal norms for all times and all places. Instead verses 11-12, like verses 9-10, were intended to curtail the influence and involvement of certain women involved in the false teachings of Ephesus.[32]

Verse 11 says, "A woman must learn in a quiet spirit with all submissiveness." The word "learn" refers to going about the business of learning. "In a quiet spirit and with submissiveness" is how they go about learning. Quiet implies a spirit of receptivity and submissiveness here refers to a willingness to be taught and to be accountable to what is taught.

The word that is translated as "try to dictate to them" or "domineer" (authentein, not exousia) is unusual and seems to have the overtones of being bossy or seizing control. That's what the Artemis women did in Ephesus. Paul is saying, like Jesus in Luke 10, that women must have the space and leisure to study and learn in their own way, not in order that they muscle in and take over the leadership as in the Artemis cult but so that men and women alike can develop whatever gifts of learning, teaching, and leadership God is giving them.[33]

In verse 12 the word "to domineer" in Greek qualifies the word "teach." So the text actually prohibits women from teaching in a domineering way. The passage is not saying that women never have authority over a man, such as existed when Priscilla taught Apollos, but that a woman is forbidden from indulging in a controlling power trip over a man, as existed in the Artemis temple at Ephesus.

What was unique here is Paul's insistence that women learn. Women were judged by Judaism to be utterly incapable of learning; no longer. In this discussion Paul was not demeaning women or putting them in a lower place but trying to get women with a hyper-elevated view of themselves to realize they are no better than men. He is leveling women with men, not demoting women beneath men.

The analogy to Genesis 3 in verse 13 was carried further in verse 14 by specifying that these Ephesian women were not to teach because they had been deceived and were transmitting false information, just as Eve was deceived and led Adam to sin. Paul's analogy says women in Ephesus were being deceived like Eve long ago. He was not saying that all women, unlike men, inherit the capacity to be deceived.[34]

Bad exegesis has led us historically to bar women from teaching men because of their supposed gullibility. Strangely enough, we historically have said that women could not hold public office or lead a business or speak in a church because they could not think straight and were easily deceived, yet we put them in charge of educating our own children at the age when their minds were most impressionable and least able to detect their errors. Does that make any sense? Such practices have always been nonsense and are now finally judged by most churches and the contemporary world to be utterly nonsensical.[35]

When Paul said that a woman was saved by childbirth, it can be interpreted that he was completely contradicting what he said in Romans 3 about salvation coming by grace through faith. If so, we are back behind the law; in fact we are taking a giant leap backward. To assert that women will be saved in childbirth makes no sense unless we know something of the myths and unsound words Paul was countering in Ephesus that demeaned marriage and childbearing. Paul was simply reminding them that being saved in Christ, marriage and motherhood go together (5:13-15 and 4:3-4).

Paul was mandating what was necessary to restore the original pattern of creation in the particular setting of Ephesus, where the original complementary relationship between men and women had been destroyed. The local heresy denied the goodness of marriage and childbearing in marriage (4:1); Paul was advocating the resumption of marriage and childbearing.

We may conclude then that 2:9-15 was addressed to a specific group of troublesome women in a particular place in the early church. The particular problem involved misinformed and domineering teachers. In overstepping traditional roles, some Ephesian women demonstrated a fundamental attitude shift that was seen in their dress and their forsaking traditionally domestic roles in a quest for a visible role in congregational life. Such domineering and assertive behavior coupled with overdressing in public certainly sent the wrong signals to Ephesus about the real nature of Christianity.[36]

Paul was concerned not with all women but with a group of women in Ephesus who were theologically unformed and morally loose, who were teaching unorthodox doctrine to the detriment of all. Paul admonished these women to be silent in order to learn from the wise teachers, the elders who teach sound words. Once they learned and brought their lives into conformity with the sound words of Scripture they would be used as they were gifted and able. The idea was not to shut up the women forever but to be silent to learn. Why would they need to learn? Not only to bless their own lives but to bless others. Women like Priscilla in Ephesus were already doing that. She and her husband Aquila had already taught Apollos.

This interpretation of 1 Timothy 2:9-15 takes into account the occasional nature of the letter, the religious myths in Ephesus, and the story and the plot of the Bible. Paul writes the 1 Timothy letter to correct the women in Ephesus. Given the background of the Ephesian women in Artemis worship or in the synagogue where they were never taught, Paul wanted these women to learn sound words (1 and 2 Timothy). For the most part they needed to learn and become mature by feeding on sound words.

Note that while the particular situation that Paul addresses in 1 Timothy arose due to particular women who were misinformed and domineering, the point of the text would be equally applicable to men who might be acting similarly.

1 Timothy 2:9-15 corrects a real problem in the Ephesian church but it does not correct the rest of the New Testament and it does not correct all women for all time.[37] It would take a huge interpretive leap to make that assumption. So when Paul was telling women to be quiet in Ephesus, it is a special kind of silence among a specified group of women in need of learning.

Silence all the time is not an interpretive option. Is it not then highly presumptuous and destructive of us to make Paul's words in 1 Timothy 2 a law for all churches for all time? Would not such an interpretation have shut up Priscilla and silenced the female prophets in Corinth and every other church in the world? Such an interpretation attempts to codify a letter into an eternal law and ignores the obvious background to this letter, the mythologies Paul references.

Carroll Osburn, a longtime professor of New Testament at Abilene Christian University, said of 1 Timothy 2:11-15:

Nothing is said in this text about informed, reliable, and gentle women teaching – either in church or out, either on religion or not, either to women or men, either to young or old. No biblical text has been so misused to dictate so many prohibitions that stifle so much service by so many people. Put simply, any female who has sufficient and accurate information may teach that information in a gentle spirit to whomever in whatever situation they may be found.[38]

GOSPEL AND CULTURE IN THE NEW TESTAMENT

Culturally the early church bent over backward to not scandalize the culture with women's liberation. In that oppressively patriarchal society, where female infants were killed if the father decided he did not want a daughter, the church was more concerned that the gospel be preached, heard, and responded to than she was that women exercise all their freedoms in the church. This is obviously part of what is going on when Paul tells women to keep their hair up to conform to the culture's standards; otherwise the culture will label these women as immoral. So Paul walked a tightrope when he speaks in these verses. He knew women were being filled with the Spirit and the gifts, and he in no way wanted to limit their ministry in the churches. Yet he wanted their exercise of the gifts to be done in a way that does not take center stage and push the gospel offstage.[39]

FIRST-CENTURY KINGDOM PERSPECTIVES

Paul expects the Lord to come in his generation. He also sees the oppressive cultural patriarchy as something he should not dismantle as his first order of business. His mission is to preach the gospel. He does not want the issue of women's role to become more important than announcing the gospel to the Roman Empire.[40] Given his obvious priorities, it would make sense for the apostle to teach a policy of social conservatism – getting along as best you can with the political powers and social structures in place in order to spread the gospel as far and as fast as possible. And they do. Paul used his liberty to fully constrain himself for the sake of the gospel (1 Corinthians 9:19-25).[41] He called his churches to do the same.

Given Paul's priority of preaching the gospel, he does two things. First, he gives the church prudent instructions on how to survive and thrive in a patriarchal culture that he thinks will not last long. This counsel is both practical and end-times oriented. Secondly, he maintains and promotes the dynamic of equality and mutuality already at work in the career of Jesus that will eventually leave gender lines behind.[42] Paul never says gifts and roles in church are gender-specific. He never says that all leaders, pastors, and evangelists should be men and that women's gifts reside among the remainder. He is not forbidding women from leadership in all circumstances and cultures. He is accommodating at certain points to the oppressive patriarchy of Judaism and the Roman Empire.

But there are certainly kingdom signs all over the place. Jesus disciples women, pours out the Spirit on them at Pentecost, promises that Spirit-gifting will be the norm in the end times, reconciles men and women together in Christ which destroys sin's curse, destroys the all-male Levitical priesthood, and gives spiritual gifts to men and women in first-century churches without regard for gender. The heart of new creation is beating within the life of the churches.

Without quenching the Spirit, the church avoided scandal and effectively fulfilled its mission in that ancient culture by accommodating the culture at certain points for the sake of the gospel. This was exactly what Paul was doing as he "became all things to all men for the sake of the gospel."

GOSPEL AND CONTEMPORARY CULTURE

In a modern culture that is egalitarian, however, the patriarchal character of the church hurts the church as she attempts to evangelize a modern and postmodern population. The scandal is that the church today is not going along with the human good that exists in this society by failing to rejoice in the unprecedented freedom women have in this society. This culture is offended, even scandalized by the church's failure to call and empower women and men to serve according to their gifts and maturity without an arbitrary gender line. This scandal impedes both the evangelism of others and the edification, retention, and development of faith of those already converted.[43]

7

Tradition – From Apostolic to Local

Our desire to understand and implement the apostolic vision must not be understood as asserting there was once a universally implemented pattern of church order that was later rejected. Paul's letters to Corinth or to Timothy were not known or read by all churches and were not understood then or now to be the defining word on church order or women. The New Testament documents show that there were other ways of ordering the communities of faith. In Jerusalem, for example, James is the leader of the church. Prophets, but not elders, are mentioned in Antioch.

So we are not attempting to restore all the practices of the New Testament church. This would amount to restoring slavery, and the wearing of veils. We do seek, however, to place ourselves under the apostolic tradition and the New Covenant Scriptures and to live faithfully to the revelation of God in Christ within our culture. We seek the illumination of the Spirit and are looking for any light from church tradition that might help us walk in faithfulness.

Tradition has to do with what has been "handed down." From the beginning we have been immersed in tradition – the handing down of the story, the worldview created by that story, and the confession of faith of those who have gone before. We can break it down into four categories: an apostolic tradition, a church tradition that began around 100 A.D., a denominational tradition (in my case, a Church of Christ tradition), and a local church tradition at Lake Highlands Church.

Jesus and the Holy Spirit commissioned and inspired the apostles, the ones sent with authority, to disciple the nations. They in turn wrote down their unique eyewitness to Jesus. The writing contained in our New Testament canon contains the apostolic tradition. We stand under the apostolic tradition that was called into existence by Jesus. When we read Scripture, we are placing ourselves under the authority of the apostolic tradition. We do not have the authority to reinvent Jesus now. We deny that latter-day revelation may contradict or be given authority over the once-for-all revelation of Jesus.

Paul speaks of the apostolic tradition he is handing down to the Corinthians (1 Corinthians 11:23ff, 15:3ff). Paul charges the church at Thessalonica to stand firm and adhere to the traditions he passed on to them (2 Thessalonians 2:1, 3:6). Since the first century the church has stood under the apostolic tradition. The Old Covenant Scriptures were included in the Christian Bible from the beginning. Early in the second century bishops such as Irenaeus contended that the four Gospels written by apostles and Paul's letters possessed authority. As time went by the Spirit caused the church to add some letters and the Apocalypse of John to the New Testament canon. This took time. The Spirit did this. All leaders in the church stand under the authority of Scripture.

CHURCH TRADITION

We acknowledge the presence, power, and leadership of the Holy Spirit throughout our 2,000-year church tradition. Therefore we have much to learn from the past – from leaders such as Augustine, Aquinas, Luther, Calvin, Wesley, and Barth – and from the creeds and practices of the church. Yet we do not stand under the church tradition; we stand with it, discerning its messages for us. The authority of the Holy Spirit and the apostolic tradition means that the historical church's creeds, leaders, practices, and councils are always secondary, always tentative, always subject to revision. Their authority is never final, never infallible, and never primary and always subject to the Spirit's and the Scripture's witness. So we read Scripture with and through tradition in a conversation that is bigger than a lifetime.

WHAT HAPPENED TO WOMEN?

Ute E. Eisen, in his book *Women Officeholders in Early Christianity*, declares that women during the first three hundred years of the church's life exercised prophetic gifts and served as presbyters, teachers, and on a few occasions, bishops. "Were there women officeholders in the church's first few centuries? The answer is yes."[44] *Ordained Women in The Early Church* by Kevin Madigan and Carolyn Isek finds evidence of women serving as deaconesses and leading churches in the West and East in the early church.[45]

When leadership involved God's choice through the gifting of the Holy Spirit, women were included. As time passed, however, church leadership was institutionalized by Rome. The empire's patriarchal culture filtered into the church and women became excluded.[46]

Aristotle said in 350 B.C. that because male is superior and female is inferior, one rules and the other is ruled. Medical doctors of the day described women as failed fetuses and men as fully developed. Galen (129-200 B.C.), the most influential medical doctor of the age, propounded these opinions as medical science. These erroneous views would rule the thinking of the West until the 20th century.[47]

Furthermore the church taught three fundamentally flawed theological assertions regarding women: they were not equally made in the image of God; they were created second and therefore were of second rank; and they were more prone to sin and deception. Thus, as a matter of creation, women were inferior to men. None of these assertions, as we have seen from examining biblical texts, can be supported by Scripture.

By the end of the fourth century the biblical vision of eschatology as the redemption of the entire creation, including the bodies of men and women, collapsed into an other-worldly vision of a disembodied heaven as the final state of the disciple. The end times was seen as an escape from the body, not the redemption of the body. Celibate asceticism, beginning in the second- and third-century church, was envisioned as the highest state of the soul on earth. Women suffered a serious setback in this bodiless vision of the kingdom of God: they were faulted for stirring up lust in men, they could not work alongside men in the church as equal partners, and they were relegated solely to the tasks of home or the calling of a female convent.

Clement of Alexandria reflected the pagan world's attitude toward women when he declared, "Every woman should blush at the thought she is a woman."[48] Gregory of Nyssa, Ambrose, and Jerome all believed that sexual intercourse was fundamentally alien to the original definition of humanity. Augustine saw continence as the highest state of spiritual life; he advocated for celibacy even for married men who became ordained. He believed it was morally impossible for women to serve or live among male clergy, even in a supporting role. The culprit for these early church fathers was the inferior woman and her body.

From 400 to 1500 A.D. the church's view of women was only marginally influenced by Scripture. Greco-Roman culture filtered into the church when Constantine brought paganism's priestly tradition into Christianity, and it affected how the church treated women. Paganism's low view of women was transmitted to the Middle Ages through Neoplatonism's hierarchical thinking. Women were low on the scale, as all rights and privileges were considered to be determined at birth through class, gender, and race. Priestly celibacy was championed in the 11th century; sex with a female somehow diminished the male's spirituality. Obviously women were considered inferior and easily deceived, and therefore unfit for any leadership over men in church, family, and society.

Thomas Aquinas taught in the 13th century, as had Aristotle earlier, that women were "misbegotten males." The medieval patterns of gender discrimination from 1100 to 1800 became codified into the laws of the state. They were tested, fine-tuned, and consolidated in Europe during that time. Consequently, women were excluded in whole or in part from social status and political power, economic opportunities and resources, civil rights and legislative due process. Stereotypes and myths of inferiority were encoded. This time period could be characterized as an era of the betrayal of women.

However, the coming of the Reformation and the Scientific Revolution did not usher in a new day for women. The new science of Francis Bacon and the new philosophies of Descartes, Kant, and Locke represented worlds without women. The rational dimension of humanity was seen as superior and was considered a masculine trait; the lesser dimensions of intuition and bodily senses were ascribed to women. It would shock Bacon and his contemporaries to know how many women are now enrolled in medical schools and law schools. Nineteenth-century preachers who were champions of women's liberation by her Lord Jesus, such as Charles Finney, were few and far between.

Women living under American democracy lacked the right to vote from 1776 until 1920. Christian leaders generally believed that a woman's reasoning ability was inferior to a man's and that the female propensity for deception made women's suffrage a dangerous idea. Christian women and men for the most part did not lead the women's suffrage movement. Horace Bushnell, a prominent 19th-century preacher, published *Women's Suffrage: Reform Against Nature*, in which he argued that allowing women to vote would lead to women developing heavier brains and ultimately to their loss of purity and morality.[49] The popular miniseries *Downton Abbey* depicts Britain in the 1920s, an era when the three Downton women cannot inherit the estate from their father. Such is the embarrassing reversal of the Jesus revolution in the West. This reversal never approached the oppressiveness of Islam but it has in large part betrayed the work of God in Jesus Christ on behalf of women.

Since the passage of the Nineteenth Amendment in 1920, America's culture of hard patriarchy has been modified dramatically. Mythologies that labeled women as inferior, unequal, evil, and unclean have been dying at an accelerating rate. Galen's so-called medical science regarding the inferiority of women and Aristotle's theory of women as misbegotten males are both dead.

Since around 1980, even Christian theologians who continue to advocate the subordination of women in church and the home no longer advocate the subordination of women in business or politics or any other public sphere. This is a dramatic break with the historic

Christian position. Neither do they argue that women are created inferior; instead they say women are equal in being to men but unequal in roles. Their reasoning, which says women are now the equals of men emotionally, intellectually, morally, and spiritually but should still have subordinate roles to men, makes no logical sense. The premise that their conclusion was built upon for 2,000 years is gone, therefore the conclusion should disappear as well.

It is more than interesting that patriarchal thinkers still argue for female subordination in the church and home but no longer in society.[50] They have rid themselves of much of patriarchy yet have held onto its practices in the church and the home.[51] So women are liberated to pursue politics and business but are held back in the home or the church. Patriarchy's belief that the subordination of women is based on the order of creation cannot be justified.

Their own interpretation demands that women must never be in a position of authority over men in any time or place, including politics and business. The idea of women holding elected or appointed positions of authority in these public spheres grievously violates the so-called God-ordained subordination of women that they contend is ironed into the order of creation.

Some want to argue that as Jesus Christ is eternally subordinate to the Father, so are women to men. The theological reality is that classical Christian orthodoxy from Athanasius to Augustine has argued that Jesus was temporarily subordinate to the Father in the incarnation based on John 1 and Philippians 2, but otherwise is not subordinate to the Father.[52]

TRADITION – PUPPY BECOMES DOG OR CAT?

What has been handed down to us is a tradition regarding women in the church that is disengaged from the dynamics of Christ's liberation of us all. Whether it is the Roman Catholic Church's exclusion of women from the priesthood, the evangelicals' argument for an exclusively male senior pastor, or the Church of Christ's struggle over women passing out the Lord's Supper, powerful church traditions oppose any change.

These issues are buried beneath multiple layers of traditionalism going back to the first century. The idea that women cannot administer the sacraments or shepherd the shepherdless is incomprehensible to anyone outside the church, and reviewing texts of Scripture would not help them understand what the fuss is all about. That's because it is about traditionalism, practices that have taken on authority unrelated to Christ or the apostolic tradition. It is impossible to escape the inertia of this powerful traditionalism without the help of the Holy Spirit.

Suffice it to say that we often are reading Scripture through the lens of our own traditions yet we are deceived into thinking that our interpretation is not colored by those traditions. We think we are standing up for the Bible, when in fact we are standing up for our traditional readings of the Bible.

John Henry Newman, the great 19th-century Roman Catholic leader, argued in his essay on the development of Christian doctrine that the growth of Christian doctrine, ritual, and practices are best understood through the analogy of organic growth. Echoing Newman and defending his theory, G.K. Chesterton quipped: "When we say that a puppy developed into a dog, we do not mean that his growth is a gradual compromise with a cat; we mean he becomes more doggy and not less. The original seed, following the biological analogy, has within itself all the later developments that will take place."[53] Only the form or experience changes, not the original seed or idea. As I. Howard Marshall has said, "developments ... must be based on continuity with the faith once given to God's people, and must be in accordance with what we have called the mind of Christ."[54]

Applying Chesterton's imagery to the issue of women's place in the church, the "puppy" (liberation of women by Jesus Christ) has been shot in the head and left for dead within much of Christian tradition. The fact that the "puppy" is still alive is a testament to the power of the Spirit in the church. Church tradition was so oblivious to this liberation that at times the puppy almost morphed into being an oppressive cat. The "puppy" has been making a comeback in recent times all over the planet. Praise the Lord!

INTO THE VOID

The women's rights movement of the 1960s brought to the nation's attention the injustice of unequal pay for equal work, sexual discrimination of women on the job, and unequal rights for women. The civil rights legislation of the 1960s led to every school in the U.S. – from elementary through college – establishing women's sports programs. Today more women than men are enrolled in higher education institutions.

I reject the philosophical foundation of secular feminism, which argues that the entire biblical worldview must be thrown out in order to liberate women. However, I acknowledge that it is the church's failure to live out the liberation Jesus provides that has opened the door for secular feminism to walk in and do many works that the church should already have done.

REAFFIRMING FAITH IN THE CHAOS

Revival and renewal in the Spirit does not only break through gender distinctions, it also calls into question barriers of socio-economic class and professionalization. Millions of women with no seminary education are currently pastoring house churches all over China. What does this mean? It can only be understood through the lens of Pentecost. Only the recovery of the Spirit and the missional trajectory of the Spirit's work in the Book of Acts give us the answer.

We reaffirm the authority of the apostolic tradition and the Holy Spirit. Yet the church does not often experience the true principle of authority – the illuminating Spirit under Christ's total authority. The Reformation principle of authority is two-fold: an external principle (the inspired Scripture) and an internal principle (the witness of the Holy Spirit), both of which are lived out within Christian community in dialogue with the entire Christian tradition.

Church traditions may help us discern God's will but they never compete with the Spirit and the apostolic tradition. Traditional readings of Scripture must be rigorously and spiritually tested in every generation, and so lead us to continual reformation and redemptive movement toward the prize of the high calling in Christ.

WHERE ARE WE NOW?

For years we as a church have been praying, reading Scripture, and listening to the witness of the Spirit in the men and women of the people of God (Acts 11-15). The Spirit has changed the culture of our local church from one of inertia regarding women's roles to one of expectancy that God is raising up women as well as men to advance the gospel of the kingdom. We are walking out the promise of Scripture and the trajectory the Spirit gives us in Scripture's story.

Our reading of Scripture has confirmed our reading of the Spirit in the church. The fruit of the Spirit has blessed the Lord's work through the women who have taught, preached, led home churches, and become youth and college pastors. The work of the Spirit in these women has confirmed the Spirit's witness in them. The result is the church has been strengthened, edified, and mobilized.

8

Hermeneutics – How Do We Get From Then to Now?

Because the idea of Scripture as a constitution or code book persists among Bible-loving Christians, many of us see the authority of Scripture appropriated to us in today's church as command, example, and necessary inference. The usual drill is to look for commands, note the examples, and make our own inferences. Something like this is practiced widely within all evangelical churches. So if you find a clear statement or two in the New Testament that tells women to be quiet, they are to be quiet. The redemptive work of Christ and the gifting of the Spirit as well as the story of women within Scripture, beginning in Genesis, are largely ignored.

But this interpretive scheme that arose in the 19th-century Stone Campbell movement flunked two big tests almost immediately: the issue of slavery in the social order and that of instrumental music in the corporate worship of the church. How does the church oppose slavery in 19th-century America if the only way she appropriates the authority of Scripture to the life of the church is through command, example, and necessary inference? After all, the New Covenant Scriptures clearly say, "Slaves, be obedient to your masters." Since there are no examples otherwise, the necessary inference is that slavery is the will of God.

If there is no command or example that authorizes instrumental music in the corporate worship of the church, how can the church justify the use of musical instruments in the church? Churches of Christ that did not use instrumental music to accompany their congregational singing insisted that instrumental music in Christian assemblies was a sinful, unauthorized addition and therefore an act of disobedience. Our pattern of discernment – command, example, and necessary inference – excluded instrumental music because the command was to sing. There was no command to include an instrument and there was no example of anyone in the New Testament era singing in a Christian assembly with instruments such as harps. So the inference was that acapella music is the will of God.

Any examination of this pattern of discernment reveals its inadequacy as the primary way to discern God's will for us. The New Covenant Scriptures suggest that commandments alone will never constitute our primary pattern of discernment. Law is good, according to Paul, but it cannot save us, and standing alone, it cannot discern God's will for us today. The New Testament from beginning to end is about gospel, not law.

Paul in his letter to Corinth certainly moved away from a legal vision of the kingdom of God. When resisting those who argue for a legal justification for their actions, Paul says: "All is lawful, but not helpful. All is lawful, but I will not be under the authority of anything" (I Corinthians 6:12). In every case Paul says the legal question is inadequate and argues that we need to ask better questions. So in 1 Corinthians he instead helps the Corinthians to ask: Is it helpful? Is it an act that will lead us into bondage? Is it consistent with our identity as Christ's body? Is it consistent with our identity as temples of the Holy Spirit? Does it advance the proclamation of the gospel? These are the questions of freedom and mission.

I have found it helpful to read the writings of brothers and sisters running on the same track and grappling with many of the same dilemmas. The journey of Carroll Osburn and Tom Olbricht within the denomination of my childhood and early adulthood helps me run the race. Almost 20 years ago, Olbricht said that after all the exegetical work had been done, confusion still persists as to the extent to which these new insights are to be incorporated into the life of the church.[55] What are we to do with the results? Careful exegetical work by itself does not always furnish clear guidelines as to how we answer this question.[56]

Olbricht recognized that our prior interpretive commitments always influence the way we relate biblical exegesis to what we actually do. For example, the exegesis of Deborah's leadership of Israel may be accurate, yet the implications for Christian leadership today are minimal for churches that discount Deborah's significance since she lived in the Old Testament period. Furthermore, Churches that do not believe spiritual gifts exist today usually discount Scriptures about women being gifted by the Lord either to lead Israel or to prophesy in an assembly. When we view as a temporary phenomenon what the New Covenant Scriptures declared regarding the role of women in the church, we tend to discount or even completely ignore the Spirit's witness in women who testify today of God's call on them and demonstrate his gifts.

AN INTERPRETIVE CRISIS

Olbricht, the most influential Bible interpreter within the Church of Christ for the last four decades, said in 1993 that the movement regarding the role of women in the church was in the middle of an interpretive crisis, without adequate interpretive guidelines by which to discerningly judge these new directions.[57] He understood 1 Corinthians 14:34-35 and 1 Timothy 2:11-15 as being directed to specific situations involving aberrant behavior and not necessitating universal silence. He also discerned the interpretive model of command, example, and necessary inference as fundamentally flawed and separated from the Bible's storyline. He believed this old model, dominated by a legal and rational grid, could not adequately discern the new directions of the Spirit within today's church.

This explains why Carroll Osburn, a prominent New Testament scholar and longtime professor at Abilene Christian University, noted that while all the evangelists and elders named in the New Testament are male, he refused to label these examples and commands as normative for today's church. Instead he simply said: "This situation should not be viewed as a pattern mandatory for all times and places, but merely as reflecting the culture in which the New Testament events were played out. Scripture does not teach that women cannot preach or serve in a leadership capacity."[58] Commands and examples disconnected from the storyline of Scripture do not carry authority for today's church. Osburn refused to make the same interpretive mistakes that supported slavery and acapella music as the will of God for today's church.

So Olbricht, aware of the "black hole" Osburn refused to fall into, asks how we move from the exegesis of the ancient Scripture to the life of the church today. What is the word of God within these texts for the church today? How do we get from then to now? Where is the energy to do something about it? In his 1996 book, *Hearing God's Voice*, he sketched a response to his own questions:

> If we are seeking a method of interpretation which comes from the New Covenant Scriptures, we might first ask who God is and what he has done and what he is reportedly doing in the world through his Spirit? What is it we are authorized to do in the church? What God has already done and is doing. This is why we are baptized – because Christ has already died and we emulate what God has done and disclose what he has done (Romans 6:1-3).[59]

If we ask who God is and consider what he has done and what he is doing regarding women, we focus the question in a biblical direction. We will not begin with a logical construct but with God.

Moving away from the Bible as a codebook or a collection of facts to be somehow interpreted by the church, Olbricht describes the Bible's storyline as the story of the Father, Son, and Spirit, and the creator of the world redeeming his fallen world. Within that story, the God who redeems and calls a people for his name expects his people to do what he is already doing in the story. Much of Scripture consists of narrative and interpretation of the meaning of that narrative. Within the narrative there are commands and examples embedded in the story. The Bible assumes the narrative is central to knowing the biblical God, for he is chiefly known through his mighty acts in history and their interpretation.

Given the finished reconciling work of God in Jesus Christ the Lord, the presence of the Spirit in all who call on the Lord, and the recovery of the Genesis 1 vision of two divine image-bearers called together to rule over creation, Olbricht answers the question about what we are to do now with another question: What textual basis remains to forbid women from serving in any capacity, especially since on occasion women such as Deborah did so with divine approval?"[60] He is concluding that we simply recognize now what God is already doing in women and release them into his work.

THE NORMATIVE VISION

If we acknowledge as normative Paul's declaration that in the Messiah "there is neither Jew nor Greek, slave nor free, male nor female, you are one in Christ," we clearly see the first pair of Jew and Greek being implemented in the actual life and structure of the New Testament church. When it comes to the second pair, slave and free, there are slight and indecisive signs of the implications involved. But the church has since made huge gains toward the liberation of the slaves all over the world. What about the third pair of male and female, the one with which we are particularly concerned in this study? We contend that all three pairs have the same potential to be implemented in the life and structure of the church, and that we cannot dispose of the third by confining it to the realm of the presence of God.[61]

Perhaps the most we can safely say is that Paul is expressing the end-point of the historical trajectory we have been tracing from the male-dominated and sometimes oppressively patriarchal society of the Old Testament, through the revolutionary implications and still-limited out-working of Jesus' attitude to women, and on to the increasing prominence of women in the apostolic church and in its active ministry.

At each point in biblical history, working out the equality expressed in Galatians 3:28 was constrained by the realities of the time and yet the church was increasingly discovering that in Christ there was the basis, indeed the imperative, to dismantle the sexual discrimination that had prevailed since the fall. How far along that trajectory the church will move is a matter for debate. But the witness of the New Testament challenges us to question any aspect of our common life in Christ that does not give appropriate expression in our day and social context to the principle that there is no longer male and female.[62]

Should not the occasional corrective words of 1 Corinthians 14 and 1 Timothy 2 be interpreted by Galatians 3:28? We are moved by the wider pattern and vision of Galatians 3:28 – a way of working out the wider purposes of God in Christ that first-century patriarchy did not allow. Galatians 3:28 declares that Jew-Gentile, slave-free, and male-female are all one in Christ; all who are in Christ are one and are of equal value. The cultural categories continue but they do not confer identity. Given the passage's import and the fact that the notion of female inferiority has been demolished, it is difficult to see how female subordination can be supported. Galatians 3:28 is not fundamentally about social liberation from cultural barriers but carries within it the seeds of transformative change consistent with our mutual identities in Christ.

WHERE IS THE BURDEN OF PROOF?

So given what the Spirit was doing at Pentecost and is doing now in Christ, where does the burden of proof lie? I find myself marshalling the arguments for the emancipation of women for whatever ministry they are gifted to do, but should the burden be on the emancipation side? I think not. The clear statements of women as co-equal, divine image-bearers, the fact that Jesus' discipled women as he did men, the declaration that the Spirit is being poured out on all – male and female – who call on the name of the Lord at Pentecost, and Paul's words, "there is neither male nor female, you are all one in Christ," place us in a new status of liberation in Christ together as men and women filled with the Spirit.

After his exhaustive examination of the Bible's storyline regarding women and the Spirit's liberation trajectory, Osburn concludes, "Restrictions against women in leadership or public ministry roles, then and now, are dictated by culture and custom rather than biblical necessity."[63]

Again I am reminded of Deborah and Huldah, raised up in the Old Covenant dispensation to lead Israel in a time of limited Spirit-indwelling and before the liberation of men and women from the conditions and consequences of sin. How could it be that women in our day, when the Spirit indwells all believers, would not continue doing the same and much more? How can it be true that we will do works greater than Jesus if only half of us can do them?

So whomever the Lord is raising up in this culture to do his work, empowered by the Spirit and grounded in the gospel, they are set free for that work. The burden of proof is on those who would restrict women from doing what God has raised them up to do. The time is short; the fields are white for harvest and the laborers are few. Why would we take seriously the call of God on half the church and ignore the other half? Israel did not argue with the Lord when he raised up Deborah, they just submitted. It's time for us to do the same.

The church needs to evidence the Christian mindset of justice, mercy, peace, patience, unity, and hospitality. We in the Spirit must be looking for equity that will allow all persons the opportunity to fashion their own lives free from existing stereotypes.[64] There are significant differences between men and women. Yet these diverse qualities should be embraced and used to enrich leadership in the church, not to exclude half the church from leadership. Women and men are magnificently distinctive and offer complementary gifts for leadership, people-keeping, and earth-keeping.

This means that the search for biblical truth is vital, that God as Father, Son, and Spirit lives within the church, that the fruit of the Spirit reign supreme, that the church is still central to God's plan, that mutual submission is basic to male/female relationships, and that women liberated by the Lord Jesus and gifted for his work should have the same opportunities to serve and lead as do men.[65]

What is at stake here is whether we reach an understanding that will permit men and women alike to become whatever it is that God intended in the beginning. Egalitarianism is preferable to patriarchy in terms of exegesis and the ideals of the kingdom. The principal concern here is to recover the egalitarian view of women that God had in mind in the creation. This means the recovery of the biblical ideal of women should evidence itself in all areas of life.

9

What About Homosexuality, Abortion, and Slavery?

We believe Jesus is Lord. We believe in the authority and inspiration of Scripture. We also believe in the Spirit's power to illuminate Scripture and help us embody the first-century word in the 21st century. We believe God is raising up men and women to do his work. The argument in this book is based on the authority of Jesus as Lord as the interpretive center of the Bible. The position articulated here acknowledges the inspiration and authority of both the Old and New Testaments, with Jesus Christ being the glue that holds the biblical story together.

I say all this to make clear that our position regarding women in the church does not indicate a wave of "liberal" change. The position contained in this argument does not embrace the gay or secular feminism's agenda, which seeks to blur the distinctions between masculinity and femininity and leave us with a unisex vision of human sexuality. That agenda is in obvious conflict with the Genesis vision of the created polarity of the sexes.

Neither does it affirm the "right to choose" position on abortion as an inalienable right of the mother. Granting a woman full rights over her own body, a central and valid concern recognized by all sensible people, should never extend to granting her full rights over another person's body, the female or male child she carries in pregnancy. Quibbling over whether the child within the mother is a person in every sense of the word obscures the fact that life has begun in some fundamentally sacred way, and that short of a miscarriage or an abortion will lead to the birth of a person with a name. Scripture has always reflected the Lord's passionate concern for the helpless and the powerless. This perspective has been lost in the agenda of secular feminism, which for the most part is not rooted in a biblical worldview.[66]

The claim that having women in leadership would open up the church to having to ordain homosexuals to ministry has no warrant in Scripture. There is one uniform position on homosexuality in Scripture from Genesis 1:1 to Revelation 22. There is nothing compelling us in the story Scripture tells to affirm homosexual acts as actions "worthy of the calling" to follow Jesus. There is not one Scripture declaring homosexual acts to be expressive of a covenant relationship with God. Homosexuality is not present in the creation narrative of Genesis, women are. This is not a matter of playing fast and loose on the texts about women and then doing the same with the texts regarding homosexuality.

But conversely, neither are we to preserve the gender roles of the Industrial Revolution simply to protect people's sexuality. Maintaining strict social differences, such as "only men work outside the home" and "women nurture children," will not protect sexual differences. Men who take care of children are not effeminate; women who work for a paycheck are not in danger of losing their femininity. Scripture calls both men and women to bring up their children in the nurture and instruction of the Lord. Both also are called to build culture together.

Examining Scripture in the Spirit will always keep us humble and penitent. Pastoring, leading, discussing, and living out the will of God in a local church on these issues clarifies what the real issues are and allays the fear that we are rebelling against the Lord's authority.

ISSUE OF SLAVERY IN SCRIPTURE

The most parallel issue we can find to women in Scripture is that of slavery. It is helpful to consider the issue of another century, see the interpretive issues involved, and then return to the issue of women in the church today. The right to ownership of another human being that existed under Roman law and under American law in the 1860s violates the biblical vision of humankind in the first chapter of Scripture.

All humans, not just the Jews and males, are divine image-bearers. All are given this inalienable identity by their Creator.

Paul possessed no power as an apostle of Jesus to liberate the slaves of the Roman Empire, so he simply says, "Slaves, be obedient to your masters." He then proceeds, however, to redefine their relationship to each other by admonishing the slaveholder to treat their slaves as he has admonished the slaves to treat their masters. He tells them not to threaten their slaves. He accommodates the cultural presence of slavery but then undermines it as an institution by redefining their relationship as brothers and sisters in the Lord, calling them to justice and kindness toward each other (see Philemon).

Paul's vision of Christ as the redeemer from human bondage was largely ignored in the South in the years leading up to the Civil War. Instead Paul's words "let slaves be obedient to their masters" were used to justify slavery again and again. The culture of 19th-century America was far removed from the Roman Empire of 60 A.D. The economics of North America was a capitalism built on contractual relationships. The political system was a democracy supported by a Declaration of Independence that had already declared all men created equal. The economics of free will contracts were far more consistent with our shared identity as divine image-bearers than was a slave-master economy.

Yet we still used New Testament commands to justify slavery. This became what historian Mark Noll refers to in the title of his book, *The Theological Crisis of the Civil War*. It took Yankee military generals to destroy the bondage of African slaves, which was defended by the church in the South. The 19th-century, Bible-believing church in America failed to liberate African slaves on theological grounds as fellow divine image-bearers, redeemed by Jesus Christ from the slavery of sin, and fellow members of the body of Christ. The church failed to discern the patterns and the trajectory of liberation within the New Covenant Scriptures.

The same interpretive arguments used now to silence women were used to enslave African Americans in 1861. Our failure of discernment concerning New Covenant Scriptures leads many in the church to silence women today. There were many in 1860 who opposed liberating the slaves because they were afraid it would also lead to the vote for women. They discerned correctly the similarity of the arguments against abolitionism and the women's vote.

Passages such as Colossians 3:22-24, Ephesians 6:5 and 7, 1 Timothy 6:1-2, and I Peter 2:18-20 all required slaves to obey their masters as they obey the Lord. In Ephesians 6 and Colossians 3, Paul gives no hint that he thinks slavery is evil. Yet however firm the biblical ties that bound slaves to their masters, virtually every modern Christian believes those texts no longer apply to us. What is crucial to see is that the interpretive justification for such redemptive movement regarding slavery will be impressively similar to the justification for rejecting gender subordination as God's Word for today's church.

In both cases, we would look for justification in the bigger pattern of events involving Christ and the Spirit, as well as the significance of these events, which give us strong leading as to the direction of God's redemptive program.

Jesus was sent "to proclaim freedom for the prisoners and ... to release the oppressed" (Luke 4:18). At Pentecost, sons and daughters and male and female slaves are all inspired to proclaim God's word. Worldly people may suppress women, yet "in the Lord ... woman is not independent of man, nor is man independent of woman" (1 Corinthians 11:11). Devout Jewish men may have thanked God every morning that they were not a Gentile, a slave, or a woman, but in Christ the subordination ironed into these distinctions has been rendered antique.

The interpretive pattern of discernment for choosing the big patterns and overall trajectory of the New Testament over the smaller, older, temporal, and local commands will be subtle. But that's nothing against it. The upshot is that it was remarkably hard in 1861 to dismiss what Paul said to slaves. The church needed an interpretive pattern of discernment rooted in a powerful, liberation narrative in order to do it. The church needs one just like that for the gender issues she faces now. We need to tell theological time. We need to see the big movement of the history of redemption that rises above the small print for local times and places.[67]

F.F. Bruce, a world-class Pauline scholar of impeccable evangelical credentials, emphasized Galatians 3:28 and kindred passages as the foundational principles of Paul's teaching in which passages on female subordination must be understood. He then wrote: "In general where there are divided opinions about the interpretation of a Pauline passage, the interpretation which runs along the line of liberty is much more likely to be true to Paul's intention than one which smacks of bondage or legalism."[68]

Given the almost universal sexism of the first-century setting, women preaching or pastoring might have been scandalous and detrimental to the preaching of the gospel. Today the situation is precisely reversed. It is the exclusion of women – often done with lofty and humorless reassurances that they are equal, even if subordinate – that is scandalous and enervating. One result is that we are hemorrhaging devout and gifted women from the body of Christ.[69]

Alongside the pain and humiliation it visits on women and the diminishment it brings to churches that drain or dam up half their talent pool, the policy of excluding women has become deeply embarrassing. Males discuss somberly whether we ought to "allow" women into church offices. The discussion sounds too much like parents trying to decide whether their adolescents are ready to assume responsibilities. It sounds so much like majorities dithering over whether they ought to invite minorities into their club. It sounds as if the church belongs to males.[70]

I know of course that decisions based on discerning the spirit, the sweep, and the direction of Scripture rather than on the "plain meaning" of individual texts make a lot of us evangelicals antsy. They make me antsy. After all, isn't that how you get theological and moral liberalism out of the Bible? Just generalize up a few levels till you get to your comfort zone and call it biblical. Haven't the Golden Rule and the love commandments been used to justify denials of the blood atonement of Jesus, acceptance of various immoralities, and interfaith dialogue in which all roads lead to heaven?

Of course. But all of us who dismissed "slaves, be obedient to your masters" as no longer the Word of God for today's church have already been walking that path. We are embarked. We reject slavery not because individual texts condemn it but because the sweep of Scripture does. Most of us evangelicals are so convinced that slavery is wicked that Ephesians 6:5 will not move us. The text must have had local and temporary application. But today we believe that if a Christian in Sudan were kidnapped, sold into slavery, and forbidden by his master to escape, his Christian duty should not be determined by reading Ephesians 6:5.

Seeing this permanently changed my mind about women in church leadership, and I'm glad it did. To me, the advent of women in church leadership has been one of the most precious gifts of God in my lifetime.[71]

Those who advocate the release of all women in Christ to live out the fullness of their calling in the power of the Holy Spirit are not calling the church to ignore Scripture's teaching any more than Christian abolitionists were calling the church in 1861 to ignore Scripture's teaching. In both instances it is a call to discern the most fundamental of all teachings within Scripture: the liberation and empowerment of us all without regard for race or gender for the work of ministry. The liberation and empowerment of women is part of the redemptive work of Jesus Christ that extends to all who call on the name of the Lord.

Christian abolitionists in 1861 were not playing fast and loose with Scripture. They were discerning the will of God for the American church as followers of the one who declared "there is neither slave nor free." Yet both the abolitionist of 1861 and the civil rights worker of 1961 were accused by the church of disturbing the church's tranquility and forcing a "liberal" political outcome on the church. Such nonsensical rhetoric is easy to see through now but it carried the day in most churches in 1861 and 1961, especially in the South.

In actual truth, abolitionism rose up out of the witness of Scripture. But as Augustine and Calvin noted, it was sometimes difficult for disciples in certain cultures to fully understand a revelation when it was granted them. Francis Asbury, the first Methodist bishop of the U.S., put it candidly in 1798: "Methodists, Baptists, and Presbyterians ... in the highest flights of rapturous piety, still maintain and defend slavery."[72] Yet Quaker abolitionist John Woolman simply quoted Matthew 25:40: "For as much as you did it unto the least of my brethren you did it to me," seeing the implication that to enslave a Negro was to enslave Christ. So the case for abolition was not rooted in a command against slavery so much as it was in discerning Christ in our brothers and sisters.

William Wilberforce led the abolition of the British slave trade because he read the Bible through the lens of the liberating, amazing grace of Jesus Christ that sets captives free. He knew the living Christ and acted to change his nation. The abolition of slavery was in Scripture but not in any command. It was there in a Person who came to set the captives free. So it is for women now.

The case against slavery and the silencing of women are theological issues. Theology includes human interpretation, and therefore sincere and brilliant seekers may reach opposite conclusions. Asbury concluded in 1798 that those who accepted slavery had drawn incorrect theological conclusions, which had neither a "sufficient sense of religion nor of liberty."[73] He contended that organized opposition to slavery arose only when and where "the appropriate moral disposition was stimulated by the salience of the phenomenon and was not counteracted by perceived self-interest."[74] It is interesting to note that the quickening of America's heart against slavery came through the witness of the Christian female writer Harriet Beecher Stowe in her novel *Uncle Tom's Cabin*, not through any book or sermon delivered by her famous father Lyman Beecher, one of the greatest preachers of the era.

Living out the promise of Scripture regarding women in the church and in society is no more ungodly or unfaithful to Scripture or to Jesus than was the emancipation proclamation of 1863. We live in a culture that is offended now when an educated female who is gifted by the Spirit is told to sit down and be quiet in the church, based only on what

Paul said in Corinthians and Timothy. Such use of Scripture misses the pattern and trajectory of the redemptive story the Bible tells. It also fails to discern in the Spirit the freedom women receive in Christ to do the work God has called them to do.

Just as we reject the idea of slavery as an institution that reflects God's will, so we reject oppressive patriarchy as an eternal word to today's church. We read the commands regarding women being silent just as we read the Scriptures telling slaves to obey their masters. We will look back one day and wonder why the church oppressed women in the same way we look back and mourn the church's support of slavery.[75]

USING THE BIBLE AGAINST GOD

The real issue as to the Bible and women is simply this: Are we telling women to be quiet by misusing the Bible as the Southern preachers did in 1860 when they used Scripture to justify slavery? They certainly quoted lots of Scripture such as, "Slaves, be obedient to your masters." I am under strong conviction that they were using the Bible against God and against his will and his intention. The texts were not placed in historical or theological context. The texts were removed from the person of Jesus Christ and the redemptive trajectory of the Scripture – from creation to fall to redemption to new heaven and new earth. The texts were used to make money off slavery. We are called to do better.

The preachers of that time who defended slavery and those of today who oppress women remind me of the eagle I witnessed recently in British Columbia. This eagle swooped down from a tree some 200 feet in the air to grab 20 pounds of salmon meat on the beach and then flew away in one continuous motion. That's how we pick and choose Scripture. We swoop down 2,000 years removed and take a text out of context and fly away with our spiritual meal for the day. But as the eagle got dead meat, so do we. Dead meat is good for eagles, but not for disciples. We are not looking for dead words jerked out of unknown contexts but for living words from the throne of God.

Harriet Beecher Stowe declared more of God's truth in her novel than thousands of preachers who delivered up dead meat to their congregations every week. She declared the living Word in the church at a time when too many preachers separated words in Scripture from the living breath of God.

The interpretive choice regarding slavery and women is between a redemptive movement or appropriation of Scripture that encourages movement beyond the original application of the text in the ancient world, or a static view that takes the words in isolation from their historical cultural context and with minimal or no emphasis on their underlying theology. The static view restricts contemporary application to how the words were applied in their original setting and can also lead to a misapplication of the text, precisely because one has failed to apply the redemptive spirit of the text in a later cultural setting.[76]

10

Pastoring the Lord's Liberation

The intentional recovery of the Spirit's work in Lake Highlands Church that began 25 years ago changed the way we saw the roles of everyone in the church, including women. We believed our experiences of the Spirit were an interpretive lens for reading the New Testament rather than an independent, counterbalancing authority. We never placed our experiences or our testimonies about what God is doing in our lives above Scripture. Yet as did the apostolic church, we reread the Scripture story to more fully understand what was happening.

We see the rudiments of this reflective process in Acts 10:34-35, where Peter begins his speech to Cornelius by alluding to Deuteronomy 10:17-18 and Psalms 15:1-2 to show that God shows no partiality, but that in every nation anyone who fears God and does what is right is acceptable to God. Peter is interpreting Scripture in the light of the work of God he has witnessed.

The Jerusalem church in Acts 15 goes through a very similar process of discernment. The witness of uncircumcised Gentiles responding in faith and being filled with the Spirit led the church back to a new reading of Scripture. This new reading discovered in texts such as Amos 9:11-12 that God's intention from the covenant with Abraham and forward was to bless all nations and to bring Gentiles to the worship of Israel's God.

To many observers, it seemed a violation of Scripture to have uncircumcised Gentiles coming into the people of God. It violated very definite Scriptures in Exodus and Deuteronomy as to the law and circumcision. Was God contradicting himself? That's impossible. So what is going on? Some said the law takes precedence over the manifest work of the Spirit; others disagreed. The Jerusalem council of Acts 15 went through a process of hearing testimony of the work of God, praying, and rereading Scripture, keeping in mind the evangelists' new experience of Gentile converts.

Scripture was in no way discarded or devalued. Rather the Spirit, in the light of this work of God, illuminated Scripture in such a way that the church over time was able to accept the decision to embrace Gentiles within the fellowship of God's people, because though it violated specific Old Testament texts, it fulfilled the promise to Abraham that through Israel the Lord would bless the nations.

These are precisely the steps that have been taken within the Lake Highlands Church regarding the role of women in the church. The challenge posed by God's activity in the church caused us to reread the Scriptures to discern what God might be doing. We were called to reread the entire story from Genesis to Revelation to become better stewards of the mystery of God's redemptive work in the world. It became apparent that the story Scripture tells points to the testimonies of women in today's church as fulfilling God's design for women as previously revealed in Scripture.

The normative vision of women in the storyline of Scripture was confirmed by the empowering of women in the early church and in today's church. Paul's corrective passages dealt with local abuses and misunderstandings but were not intended to alter in any way the normative vision of Genesis 1:27-30 and 2:24, Luke 10:38-42, Acts 2:14-36, and Galatians 3:28.

WOMEN – LIVING DESCRIPTIVE TEXTS

We have discerned God's will not by just interpreting written-down texts in the Spirit. We also discerned God's will by interpreting the Spirit's living texts, women he has gifted for service in the kingdom. Gifted women in leadership right now in the church are living descriptive texts. These women are part of a great band of witnesses stretching all the way back to Priscilla. Since 1989 I have personally witnessed the Spirit raising up women in the Lake Highlands Church to teach, preach, and pastor. I give these living texts weight, but not the weight I give Scripture. However, these living texts confirm again and again our interpretation of the Scripture texts.

As the Spirit coming on the Gentiles in Acts caused the church to reread her Scripture texts, so has the Spirit's work in women called us to reread the Scripture story to discern what is going on. In every instance the Spirit has confirmed our interpretation of the Scripture texts. The normative and descriptive texts of Scripture are perfectly consistent with what I am reading in the lives of Spirit-filled women today.

The interpretations of the past will always remain intact and even petrified without the Holy Spirit's stimulating work in today's church. The Scripture will be heard to say the same thing over and over again unless our hearing is renewed by the story inscribed among us even now by the finger of God. Without the narratives of these women, we cannot discern what God is telling us.

Let it be noted that my homosexual brothers will argue that just as God is blessing women, God also is blessing their loving homosexual relationships, and that I should give my blessing to their relationships. They are asking that I give singular authority to their experience over the witness of Scripture. I respectfully disagree. I do not give anybody's testimony countervailing authority over Scripture. I have gone to Scripture and in light of their testimony have reread Scripture, asking if in light of this testimony homosexual marriage can somehow be understood as a fulfillment of God's design for human sexuality as revealed in Scripture.

Contrasted with the biblical testimony as to women, however, the witness of Scripture is univocal in its opposition to homosexual marriage, beginning with Genesis 1 and including Jesus' words and those of the early church. The story of women in Scripture is dramatically different from the story of homosexuality, beginning with "God made humankind, male and female created he them."

Paul says in his letter to Corinth that the Spirit was blessing believers who were living unholy lives. But God's gracious presence was never understood by Paul to be a license to sin; rather it is an occasion to repent. In Romans, Paul put it simply, "Shall we continue in sin so that grace may abound?"

PASTORING THE LIBERATION OF WOMEN

Without a place to narrate the story of what women consider a call from God, how can the authenticity of that call be discerned by the church? I began to see the Holy Spirit energizing women and gifting women in the local church. It was reminiscent of Acts, but instead of Lydia, Priscilla, and Phoebe it was Keri, Diann, and Robin. How many other women in the last 2,000 years have heard a call to serve the Word but did not pursue it because no one took their story seriously enough to even listen? What about the narrative of those who were ministered to by women? It is inconceivable to me that the church would not even be interested in hearing what God has done among his people, men and women, through revelation that is only available through such narratives of faith.

So I became a minister of slow yet significant change for more than twenty years. It was the change that the Spirit brings. We adopted the early apostolic church's theological model of discerning God's patterns. I heard the witness of the church; I heard the witness of women. I was led to use the gifts of women that were already being used among women to edify the entire church. It was already happening here in 1984. Lana, a gifted Bible expositor, was teaching an adult Bible class to women but men were coming as well. Should Lana stop? Was this a work of Satan or God? Nobody seemed to ask very good questions about this back then.

Many of us grew to see that Lana had actually been doing what Paul told women to do in 1 Timothy 2: to learn Scripture. Lana learned and then taught. Given the fruit of her labors, it seemed to be what the Lord had in mind. Slowly we began asking better questions and received discernment.

As I came to strong convictions about these matters, the Spirit led me to slowly do something about it. It was part of our empowering the entire church for full-time ministry in the world. To more fully embody the end-times vision, I was led to become an equipper of women. This meant I would:

1. Attentively begin discerning the work of the Spirit in women.
2. Begin teaching and preaching on the place of women in the True Story of the world.
3. Begin using women in the church as they are gifted, not according to gender.
4. Begin using women to lead home churches, teach classes, and preach sermons as they were gifted and matured to do so.
5. Empower for leadership Spirit-filled and gifted men and women who were not professionally trained in "ministry."
6. Recognize that home-building and parenting may in fact be full-time work for women and even men.
7. Understand that wineskins and practices in the church will change as we invite all men and women to exercise their gifts according to the common good.
8. Bathe the empowerment in prayer: "Lord, reveal to us your will."

We have begun walking in the freedom Jesus brings. We have recognized and used the gifts. We have listened to the witness of women and then embodied it, and the fruit has been the Spirit's.

Keri, a woman of the Spirit who was gifted to teach and who taught other women, was asked by the pastoral leadership fifteen years ago to teach and preach to the entire church. Since then the Spirit has confirmed the gifting in women such as Keri, Diann, Robin, Donjalea, and more recently Andress, Kim, and others. These women all give testimony to the redeeming work of God in their lives, all are passionate for God, all are full of the Spirit and gifted to communicate the word of God, and all are gifted to shepherd believers and are engaged in humbly doing so as we speak.

Has the fruit of that season taught us that God was not really interested in using women? Did we find when women taught or preached or pastored that God's work was harmed in any way or was the kingdom in fact advanced? What is the Holy Spirit doing? What is the Holy Spirit's witness in and through women here in this church? The answer is that God has worked powerfully through women in their servant leadership. We did not find women striving to dominate as some had feared, but rather women who simply used their gifts and sat down in humility. The fruit was ours to judge and that is where we are now.

Several years ago Diann was raised up very suddenly and yet very obviously to become the youth pastor in our church. Such a work of God was unanticipated by everyone and yet was a great blessing to the entire church. It was a step away from the oppression I had lived through for fifty years, beginning as a 12-year-old member of the youth group. Diann pastored boys and girls as well as young men and young women from the ages of 12 to 18. After two years Diann believed herself called to pastor college students along with her husband, Phil. She resigned as the youth pastor and began teaching and pastoring college students and 20-somethings. She was and is pastoring adults. She has the gifts of teaching and pastoring as well as the passion and maturity to do the work.

Two young women in their 20s, Hayley and Jessica, led a home church that included women and men. They did it because they were gifted to do it and because the members of that group submitted to their leadership. There were no men standing in line to take their place. The same was also true of Donna and Debbie, who also led house churches full of men and women. In all these instances, women exercised pastoral leadership over a part of the church in concert with the shepherding leadership of the church.

We are walking in the "way of the Lord." The days of women being ignored are over. We are walking in the freedom and fruitfulness the Lord gave us when he encouraged Mary of Bethany to listen to him and be discipled. That's why he poured the Spirit out on men and women. He did not redeem and fill them to sit them down and never use them to prophesy, preach, or pastor. Certainly he redeemed them for a thousand other ministries that are of great importance. But why would he raise up and gift women to prophesy, preach, and pastor if in fact he actually wanted them to sit on the bench and watch a weakened, depleted, all-male team play the game?

The church is desperate for sound words from responsible and humble shepherds who will die for their sheep. Do we have too many shepherds, too many teachers, too many prophets? We know the answer. If we are to do greater works than Jesus, it will take all of the church, doing all of the works of God, all of the time. Telling half of the church they can do all the works will never get the job done.

Dallas Willard wrote, "What we lose by excluding the distinctively feminine from 'official ministries' of teaching and preaching is of incalculable value. That loss is one of a few fundamental factors that account for the astonishing weakness of 'the church' in the contemporary context."[77] Women and men are indeed very different, and those differences are essential to how God empowers each to bring the kingdom of God into their life and ministry.[78]

Let me be clear that just because a woman or a man tells me they have a gift of leadership, prophecy, or teaching does not make it so. There are many "wannabes" who never will "be" unless and until they get low and stay there. But there are many more, especially women, who are endowed and called but who have given up, who are not looking for the limelight but who know there is a need out there, and also discern a gift and calling in them that could connect but never does. They are tired of climbing over insurmountable walls. I know a young girl who asked at the dinner table, "Why can't women say the blessing?" The patriarch was silent, and the girl was ignored. No one said a word. All of the silent Christian women at that table are in bondage. How long will we remain silent in the church?

Their narrative compels us to discern what God is doing in these women. Therefore we are reading Scripture but we are also reading what the Spirit is doing in the church, including the women of the church, and then again and again rereading Scripture, praying, and begging for discernment.

We began asking different questions:

If we start with male-female, as humankind jointly responsible for stewarding the entire creation, would it be surprising to see women working right along with men in advancing the kingdom of God on this earth in the end times?

Is "ministry" a word for an elite male club or is it descriptive of a Spirit-mobilized army of the whole church?

By what authority do we say to women and to men who are gifted and mature for ministry that they are disqualified because they are the wrong gender or because they did not go to seminary and get ordained by their denomination?

Does the fact that God commanded only Jewish men to go into all the world and disciple the nations mean that Gentile women who have done this work all over the world have been disobedient in so doing?

Does the fact that God does not authorize women to shepherd by command anywhere in the New Testament mean that he would oppose such for all time in the church?

Why would God want to exclude female shepherds just because they are female? Why would he do that?

Do we already have too many shepherds in the church?

Given the appearance in Scripture of leaders such as Deborah, Junia, Phoebe, and others, what Scripture would you use to say that God is opposed to appointing a Spirit-gifted woman to a task of church leadership?

Does the command to Timothy to appoint elders imply that this letter for the Ephesian church explicitly forbids for all time appointing women to shepherding leadership?

If 42,000 a day are coming to Christ in China and are for the most part being led by female pastors in house churches, should we remove those pastors on the basis that they are female?

Should the question be "Which gender is in charge?" or "What does God want to get done?"

Do we not begin at a better place when we ask who is called, gifted, and mature rather than is this potential leader a male or a female?

GIFTS, OFFICES, AND SUCH

There is no one pattern within the New Testament of which particular churches have the franchise. Paul told Timothy in Ephesus to appoint elders, but in Antioch and Corinth the leadership appears to be charismatic prophets. In Jerusalem, James is the leader. So what is the pattern of church leadership? There is not one singular pattern given in the New Testament. What should it be now? Doesn't the Spirit answer that question?

Often believers will ask, "Can a woman be a senior pastor?" I find it interesting that we are referring to an office that is not mentioned or institutionalized in the New Covenant Scriptures. The same is true for the Roman Catholic celibate priesthood and the Episcopal bishop. None of these are described in the New Testament. So the question of whether a woman can assume an unbiblical role is not a very good question, to say the least.

In evangelical churches, "senior pastor" has become a title for anyone who preaches at a church regularly for money. But such a ministry function does not make one a senior pastor. Such a function is that of a teacher, maybe a preacher-prophet, but not necessarily a pastor. A 30-year-old man or woman who preaches every Sunday is not a biblical elder-pastor; he/she is a neophyte. And if he/she is the only pastor in the church, the church is without a shepherd. The notion that every church should have a senior pastor does not come from Scripture. Arguing over whether women should be senior pastors begins with a bad question. A better question would be, "Why not appoint women whom God is already using to shepherd disciples to be shepherds of churches?"

A church may have a senior pastor whom God has raised up, but why institutionalize this role? Then the role itself becomes part of our institutional baggage, which in turn changes the questions regarding women in ministry. I came to the church I presently serve only to preach and teach, and I did so for ten years before I became an elder. Even then I was not the senior pastor, the shepherd father of the church. After fifteen years in the church, God raised me up to be the "senior pastor" to preserve the unity of the Spirit in the church and to shepherd the church through a crisis of leadership. Becoming a senior pastor is about time together, some age, a measure of wisdom, and the trust of the sheep.

When I am finished with this calling, those much younger than I who preach and teach now in my place will not be the "senior pastor." They will be whatever they are gifted to be. Those who do not preach will assume other pastoral duties. Is God raising up men and women to assume these roles? It appears that he is. But at this moment, none to senior pastor.

So instead of asking if a woman can be a senior pastor, ask another question: Does God need male and female shepherds to do the pastoring of the men and women in the church? This question is the one that Jesus the Shepherd wants us to ask. The answer is obvious. Bill Hybels, a longtime preaching pastor at the Willow Creek Church, says:

At this point I cannot imagine doing senior leadership in a church without full participation of women at every level. I wouldn't want to make important decisions without the world and life view that women offer. You learn something by being a mom that you don't learn by being a dad. You experience something as a little girl growing up in church that you don't experience as a little boy. As church leadership teams we need to view the church family from the perspective of both genders. We need the cross-pollination of ideas that can shape better ideas for the future. I don't know how we can do this unless we have both women and men serving in every area of our ministry.[79]

Who exactly are we disobeying if we recognize as shepherds those Spirit-filled women who have attained wisdom and are already shepherding sheep on behalf of the Great Shepherd? There is a vantage point and God-given sensitivities that women bring to enrich shepherding. A woman speaking strong words to men and women is often the wisest way to shepherd sheep. Recognizing their gifts and calling gives them credibility and authority within the church.

Dallas Willard says the exclusion of women from official positions leaves women generally with the impression there is something wrong with them.

> What could it be? And if leadership, speaking, and the like are good work, and if the work is manifestly in need of good workers, what exactly is it about a woman that God sees and says: "That won't do." Or did he just flip a coin and men won? ... It is noteworthy what a hard time that those who oppose leadership by women have in saying exactly what it is about women that excludes them from such positions and how that puts an unbearable weight on what was already a very weak hermeneutic.[80]

It is impossible for me to believe today that given the hunger of women for Scripture and for the Lord, their apparent knowledge and maturity as well as Spirit-gifting, that the Lord 2,000 years later does not want to use any of them to prophesy, preach, or pastor. He is certainly using them for everything else! Maybe if there were an excess of shepherds in the church such a conclusion would be possible. But the sheep of the Lord are wandering right now as sheep without shepherds, and we want to quibble about women doing this good work. It is nonsense.

If the gifts of Spirit are not gender-sensitive, why do we not encourage a leadership team of pastors with multiple gifts and who minister out of their femininity and masculinity to more effectively shepherd the church? Are prophets, preachers, or pastors out to boss the church? Never! They are called to edify and pastor the church. The daunting task of pastoring the whole church with all of her wounds and immaturity suggests that it would be wise to have a plurality of shepherds and shepherdesses in the church.[81]

The Spirit now working through women leading house churches all over China and spreading the life of Jesus to millions indicates that sometimes the Holy Spirit just runs off and leaves the so-called institutional church. Clearly, we can do greater works in this generation than did Jesus when all of his body is freed up totally to run with the Spirit to the end!

11

What About Roles in Marriage?

I once counseled a married couple who both had very strong personalities and were locked in a power struggle. When I mentioned the word mutuality, the husband did not know what I was talking about. He was looking for a hierarchical model to make his marriage work and I was advocating a relational model. I found it a futile exercise to counsel these two as they remained locked in a bitter struggle for power.

Historically, male headship in the West has meant that husbands controlled everything in the home, including parenting, domestic questions, and business matters. When the 19th-century Industrial Revolution removed men from the home, women were pronounced queen of all that went on in the house, including parenting and running the household. The father was master of everything else, meaning he had been relegated to the role of provider. This is how the church preached and taught about marital duties throughout most of the 20th century.

Post-World War II capitalism changed all that. Women began working outside the home because the needs and wants of the family required two paychecks. Providing and parenting are now shared responsibilities in many homes. The hard patriarchy of another era has been replaced in an era of equal rights by "patriarchs" who do not make decisions without consulting their wives. If they do, their wives might resent them and feel disrespected.

The question of who is in charge seems increasingly useless. How does it actually work? In nearly all the marriages I know that practice a "soft patriarchy," the husband and wife function as two equals. The marriages that give all the say-so to one spouse do not nurture both husband and wife. Someone is disrespected and their marriages fail to thrive.

MARRIAGE, ROLES, AND GENDER

From the time of Aristotle through the second half of the 20th century, men regarded women as an inferior species and many women agreed with them. But now the Western world has reversed what used to be the assumed stereotype. Women are no longer considered inferior; in fact men sometimes must apologize for having too much testosterone. Women often want babies without husbands or fathers – in other words, without men. So we live in a time of disempowered men and unnecessary fathers.

What sociologists call the "male problematic," the passivity of men within their marriages and their families, is a much greater problem now than male domination.[82] Not only are many men not the leaders of their families, they do not function as co-equal contributors. In this problematic situation are some women who claim their husbands are heads of the house but who in fact are actually "running the show" themselves. This strange circumstance results in a seldom-acknowledged female domination. I am not an advocate of female domination any more than I am an advocate of male domination. Both fall short of the created ideal.

Our working definitions of masculinity and femininity have contributed to conflict and gender confusion in men and women. The conventional wisdom is that men don't cook or clean house, wash the dishes, or pick out colors to decorate the house. Real men love basketball, baseball, or football – otherwise there must be something wrong with them. Women should never come on as strong or able to make big decisions, and they shouldn't be able to analyze complex issues or hold down a high-pressure job. Men cannot be expected to be nurturers because, as one popular Christian writer claims, they are "wild and untamable" and must roam the countryside. The distortions multiply.

We struggle with the roles we believe God has given us. Is a stay-at-home dad a violation of Scripture? How about a stay-at-home mom? Women ask if they can have a career and be a mother. Why do men not ask the same question? Can a man have a career and also be a real father? Men were stay-at-home dads until the Industrial Revolution. The idea that women are nurturers and men are providers has hurt several generations of children. It has no basis in Scripture, which instead tells us, "Fathers bring up your children in the nurture of the Lord."

STEREOTYPES AND SIN

Are we the way we are because we were created that way or because we have been socialized a certain way? These questions are important and the answers require diligence, otherwise the stereotypes will win. We act as if women are inferior but we have no Scripture to support that. Women cannot run as fast as men or pump as much iron; in that sense women are weaker. But women, not men, are built to birth a child. Women rank ahead of men in many intellectual dimensions. It's obvious that women live longer than men do. So men are weaker than women at key junctures. I find Donna's strength very comforting, consoling, and helpful. We are partners on the same team for goodness' sake. The tug of war is over.

SO WHAT ABOUT MARRIAGE NOW?

For Jesus' disciples, marriage is shaped by the person of Jesus Christ and by both husband and wife living in the Spirit, reading Scripture, and asking, "How do I live out the vision set out in the New Covenant Scriptures in this culture?"

The first passage to examine is 1 Peter 2:18-3:4, which is set in the context of admonitions to Christians in the world:

> Slaves, accept the authority of your masters with all deference, not only those who are kind and gentle but those who are harsh ... for to this you have been called because Christ also suffered for you, leaving you an example that you should follow in his steps. ... Wives

in the same way, accept the authority of your husbands, so that even if some of them do not obey the word, they may be won over without a word by their wives' conduct when they see the purity and reverence of your lives. Do not adorn yourselves outwardly by braiding your hair, and by wearing gold ornaments or fine clothing; rather let your adornments be the inner self with the lasting beauty of a gentle and quiet spirit.

The call for submission of women in 1 Peter derives its meaning from the rest of the instructions in 1 Peter. Christian women are commanded to show deference to their disobedient husbands by avoiding behavior that would offend them or appear rebellious to them. Even believing in a God other than the God the husband believed in was considered rebellious. Braiding hair and wearing jewelry in the ancient world were understood as acts of defiance toward the husband. In a time when Christians were being accused of undermining basic institutions of society, Christian wives are called to vanquish these rumors. In 1 Peter 3, women are to submit to their husbands to witness to them of the love of Christ in an oppressively patriarchal culture. To do otherwise would destroy their witness to their husbands.

This demand on Christian wives belongs to a very different situation than our own. The command to submit belongs with the call for submission to governmental authorities and the submission of slaves to their masters. The call for submission here is grounded in the structure of ancient institutions, not the order of creation. Therefore one cannot simply transfer these instructions to our own time. The challenge to submit to governmental magistrates (2:13-17) is more functional in autocratic societies than democratic societies, where one has the opportunity for various forms of participation. Therefore instructions addressed to Christian wives in the first century cannot just simply be transferred into the modern situation.

The meanings are not the same. The ancient words of 2:18-3:4 addressed to citizens, slaves, and wives cannot be transferred to our own time without considerable reflection and translation.

Christian slaves who are abused by non-Christian masters are told to walk in Jesus' steps. The deeper intention of 1 Peter becomes apparent when one compares the words addressed to slaves in 2:21-25 with those addressed to "all" in 3:8-12. All are expected to be humble and to avoid returning evil for evil (3:8-9). As are the slaves in 2:21, the entire Christian community is called in 3:9 to a specific conduct rooted in the way of the Cross.

This deeper intention also is seen in the instructions to those who hold dominant roles in the ancient institutions. Christian husbands are called to live considerately with their wives as joint heirs of the grace of life (3:7). Those who hold authority are told not to abuse power (5:1-4). The entire church is to walk in humility. Thus the order of the ancient society is assumed in 1 Peter but is transformed by the story of the Cross.[83]

Likewise Ephesians 5:21-33 ties marriage to Christ and the church:

> Submit to one another out of reverence for Christ. Wives, submit yourselves to your own husbands as you do to the Lord. For the husband is the head of the wife as Christ is the head of the church, his body, of which he is the Savior. Now as the church submits to Christ, so also wives should submit to their husbands in everything. Husbands, love your wives, just as Christ loved the church and gave himself up for her to make her holy, cleansing her by the washing of the water through the word, and to present her to himself as a radiant church, without blemish, but holy and blameless. In this same way, husbands ought to love their wives as their own bodies. He who loves his wife loves himself. After all no one ever hated their own body, but they feed and care for their body, just as Christ does the church. For we are members of his body. "For this reason a man will leave his father and mother and be united to his wife, and the two will become one flesh." This is a profound mystery – but I am talking about Christ and the church. However, each one of you also must love his wife as he loves himself, and the wife must respect her husband.

The key to Ephesians 5 is, "Be subject to one another out of reverence for Christ." This is the only structure possible. The man is the head of the wife like Christ is head of the church, but not in exactly the same way. Christ rules as Lord of the world. No man is a lord with absolute power. Paul is not focusing on the power of Christ but on the sacrificial death of Christ as an example to be followed. The text does not mention a man ruling or governing; all are told to submit. Children and slaves are told to obey, not the wives.

The backdrop of everything Paul and Peter are saying in these passages about men, women, slaves, and children is Aristotle's ancient household theory: the tyrannical rule of master over slave, the aristocratic rule of husband over wife, and the monarchical rule of father over children. As to the relationship of husband over wife, "man rules in accordance with his worth."[84]

When discussing gender roles, Paul uses Jesus as his model, not the bossy or bullying male of modern or ancient time. He says the church is the bride of Christ, not because she was abducted but because he gave himself totally and voluntarily for her. It was Christ's complete self-giving, self-abandoning love that drew the church to respond in kind.

Paul, of course, lived in a world where women were not only regarded as inferior but also as unclean. Their bodily functions were thought to make them dangerous for a man who wanted to maintain his own purity. The husband, by contrast here, is to assist in bringing the wife into full purity. Instead of rejecting the wife at times of technical impurity, the husband is to cherish and take care of her, and to let her know at all times that she is loved and valued.

But let's go a little deeper into the text and the times as we listen for God's leading. First is the radical injunction for a husband and wife to mutually "submit to one another out of reverence for Christ" (5:21). This precedes and frames the words asking wives to be subject to their husbands (verse 22). Aristotle spoke of a proportional equity: man rules in accordance to his worth and an aristocracy of the husband over the wife is based on superior worth. There is no mutual subjection because Aristotle does not believe women are divine image-bearers, as are men. Remember, he believes women are misbegotten males. Paul disagrees on all points.

Second, Ephesians tells husbands to love their wives as Christ loves the church. Aristotle based his concept of proportional equity on what he considered the higher deliberative powers of men. He believed the male is by nature fitter for command than the female. Marriage for the ancient world was not about love. Paul disagrees, and calls all men to emulate Christ, who is the new model of masculinity.

Third, Ephesians tells husbands to love their wives as Christ loves the church, thereby developing a theory of male servitude. Three times in 5:25-33 the husband is told to love his wife, and this love is to be demonstrated in the same way that Christ loves the church. Loving wives in the same way as Christ loves the church points to service, not power. The entire vision of mutual deference was a new way of relating. Nothing is said about decision-making or gender roles. Paul turns upside down Aristotle's idea that the higher value within a marriage goes to the man who, because of his greater virtue, deservedly gets more of what is good.[85]

Several years before Paul wrote Ephesians, he had instructed the Corinthians that in Christ the husband belongs to the wife in the very same way that the wife belongs to the husband (7:2-5). He also discussed divorce and remarriage, using the same criteria for women as he did for men (7:2-16). What Paul and Peter said may be objectionable to 21st-century believers in an egalitarian culture but their teaching on these matters transformed the minds of those believers living in a society of unrestrained hard patriarchy.

We can neither dismiss the ancient instructions in 1 Peter and Ephesians as cultural relics of the past nor uncritically adopt them as commandments for our own time. While submission is not rooted in the order of nature, it cannot be cast aside because it is rooted in the Cross (1 Peter 2:21-25). This is what the call to submission actually meant in New Testament times.

But we ask the hermeneutical question as well: how do commandments given within a specific social ethos function in a society that has changed? If the call in the New Testament for women to submit in the marriage relationship was actually a challenge to fit in with the cultural expectations of that time, how do Christians appropriate this commandment today?

If the deeper intention of 1 Peter is to call Christians to follow Jesus within the institutional expectations of their time, the challenge to the contemporary church is to follow Jesus not by transferring ancient views of authority to our own time but by recognizing that those who follow Jesus reject the pursuit of power and the will to dominate. Thus in submitting to their husbands, Christian wives continue to walk in the steps of the crucified one. However, since the call for submission is rooted in the story of the Cross, the Christian husband is also called in the modern situation to share with his wife in reciprocal submission.[86]

Clearly there are significant differences between men and women that go beyond biology and reproductive function. From the beginning, we have complementing sensibilities. I reject the feminist notion that other than reproductive differences, male and female are constitutionally the same. There are differences, but none that make one a leader all the time and the other a follower all the time. Neither are men and women in Christ given gifts that are gender-exclusive and only to be used by someone either in leading or following.

What seems so obvious to me after forty-six years of marriage is that men and women as Jesus' disciples are called at times to lead and at times to follow their spouse as they both practice mutual submission and reciprocal living. Passive men must step up to this challenge as must passive women. Domineering women as well as domineering men must step down to this challenge, guided every step of the way by Jesus Christ who gave himself up for the church.

In a time of male passivity, men must hear the call to lead. But this in no way means women are not called to lead. Because of the creational differences and the diverse spiritual gifting, both men and women will lead in different marital circumstances. Their leadership styles will be very different and this diversity will bless the marriage.

It makes no sense today to say anything else. All of us lead as did Jesus Christ, who sacrificed himself for us. We lead in meeting needs and in mutually sacrificing ourselves for each other. We rhythmically take turns leading each other through a day, then a week, and a year. We continually complement each other. The question of who is in charge never comes up. Shaping all of this is the call on both husband and wife to mutually submit to each other. So every good marriage has two leaders and two followers, both mutually submitted to Christ. Nothing else really works.

All of this may sound contradictory; it is not. It is paradoxical, however, with two seemingly contradictory statements and yet both are true because of the greater truth, that Jesus who is Lord "did not count equality with God a thing to be grasped but emptied himself."

We are doing marriage now in a very different way than did our forefathers. Every couple I know in the church either practices what I would call "soft patriarchy" or a purely egalitarian marriage defined by mutuality. The first option says the parties to the marriage discuss every decision in the marriage with mutual respect for each other, and if they cannot reach an agreement, the husband casts the tie-breaking vote. The second option says the parties equally submit to one another out of reverence for Christ. Decisions are made by the parties submitting themselves to the will of God.

My marriage to Donna is characterized by the egalitarian model. I think it better reflects the will of God for us. It's the only model I know how to do in the name of Jesus. If I actually believed Donna was subordinate and inferior to me, why would I ever give what she thinks any weight? If I am lord of the house, when does Donna make any decision, however small, without my prior approval, and why do I have to ask her opinion before making any decision, however great or small? The questions themselves are repugnant and no longer a part of my life.

I cannot imagine living with my wife in a marriage that was anything other than an equal-regard marriage based on our joint call to be divine image-bearers. We are called to co-equal, divine image-bearing.

We do not manage separate spheres, where women are angels of the home and men are captains of industry. Women are not told to be fruitful and multiply, and men are not told to subdue the earth. Both receive the cultural mandate and both are responsible for so doing.

The Spirit is working in our marriages to help us discern truth that we missed in Scripture. When I got married, I saw myself as C.S. Lewis saw himself when he got married. Marriage was a hierarchical relationship with me at the top of the mountain. Lewis was never accused of being a feminist, but in his book *A Grief Observed*, written after Joy's death, he commented on what he learned about masculinity and femininity in an intimate marriage:

> There is, hidden or flaunted, a sword between the sexes till an entire marriage reconciles them. It is arrogance in us to call frankness, fairness and chivalry "masculine" when we see them in a woman: it is arrogance in them to describe a man's sensitiveness or tact or tenderness as "feminine." But also what poor warped fragments of humanity most mere men must be to make the implications of that arrogance plausible. Marriage heals this. Jointly the two become fully human. In the image of God created he them. Thus by a paradox, this carnival of sexuality leads us out beyond our sexes.[87]

Being married moved Lewis from a hierarchical model to a mutuality model. So it was for me, thirty years later. I had no idea how much I was starved to become fully human with Donna in a relationship of mutual equality and intimacy.

Concluding Reflections

IMPROVED PATTERNS OF DISCERNMENT

Using the entire Scripture and being energized by the Spirit's renewal 25 years ago, our church began a more discerning read of the entire canon's witness to women in the True Story of the world. Our interpretive discernment was improved by:

1. Claiming the entire Bible from Genesis 1 to Revelation 22 as the Word of God, the True Story of the world. Regarding women, we started not with the "shut up" passages but with creation, and with male and female as co-equal, one-flesh divine image-bearers.
2. Placing the domination and manipulation between the sexes in the story of the fall, not as the divine intention for creation.
3. Recognizing the Lord's accommodation to sin in the Mosaic law but also noting that the Spirit of God sovereignly acted to raise up Miriam as a prophetess, Deborah as a judge, and Huldah as a prophetess. Yet the story ground on into oppressive patriarchy, demeaning and devaluing women until the time of Jesus.
4. Placing at the center of our patterns of discernment the stunning, unique work of Jesus Christ the Lord, redeemer and discipler of women as well as men. All that the Lord God is and has done for us and the whole world is given priority well above any particular word, however inspired or important, spoken by anybody else.

5. Giving the Spirit's outpouring at Pentecost on all in Christ without regard for gender its place of critical importance for the life of the church. The issue of women's role is no longer an issue of gender but of Spirit-gifting. The significance of this Spirit action, which continues today in the church, changes not only the answers but the question: By what authority does any man restrict a Spirit-gifted woman from exercising her gifts? Because the Spirit is filling and gifting the church now as he did on Pentecost, we hear and discern the witness of women regarding the Spirit's work in them; they are no longer ignored. So we read both Scripture and the Spirit in the church today.

6. Interpreting Paul in the light of what Jesus has done and the trajectory of freedom that the work of Jesus and the Spirit brings to the world. Paul's corrective words to women are read in context as corrections of abuses in two local churches, not corrections of what Jesus has already done and is doing in the world. Otherwise we must say that Priscilla, Junia, and the prophetesses at Corinth were disobeying God when they prophesied, worked as apostles, and served with authority in the presence of men.

7. Continuing to acknowledge the historical distance between the first and the 20th centuries but also reclaiming our place in the story the New Covenant Scriptures tell —and our life in the same act of the same play, the age of the church, created by the Spirit of God for God's end-times purposes – produces humility and confidence in us.

8. Accessing God's will for today's church by knowing who God is, what he has done, what he is doing now, and who we are now as a result of what he has done. We are called to do what he is doing. The story calls us to be Spirit-filled improvisers, living faithfully to the vision revealed to us in the Scriptures within the cultures of our time. We reject all legalistic grids, including commands, examples, and necessary inference. Yet we also honor the commands of the Lord embedded in the True Story

of the world as possessing transcultural authority, including "Love each other as I have loved you" and "Present your body as a living sacrifice, holy and acceptable to God."

9. Recognizing that the redemptive movement within the story Scripture tells gives us a way to "handle the Bible aright." Had the early church lived out the fullness of what God had done in the world? Certainly not. "We are to do greater works than he did." The story has redemptive-movement dynamics all the way through. Yet at no point can we say we have arrived. This is not only true for Israel; it is true for the church. We are looking for signs and trajectories that tell us, in light of who God is and what he has done, where we are to go.

10. Mobilizing the entire church to do kingdom work according to how we are gifted, without regard for gender. Only in this way will the church be fully matured and mobilized to embody Christ's transformative presence in the world.

Notes

1. Dallas Willard, *How I Changed My Mind About Women in Leadership*, ed. by Alan Johnson (Grand Rapids: Zondervan, 2010) 10.

2. Quoted in Alice Matthews, "Toward Reconciliation" in *Discovering Biblical Equality*, eds. Ronald W. Pierce and Rebecca Groothius (Downers Grove, Illinois: InterVarsity Press, 2004) 496.

3. John Stackhouse, *Finally Feminist* (Grand Rapids: Baker Academic, 2005) 28.

4. G.K. Chesterton, "Why I Am a Catholic," Internet site.

5. Scott McKnight, *The Blue Parakeet* (Grand Rapids: Zondervan, 2008) 87-91.

6. Carroll Osburn, *Women in the Church* (Abilene, Texas: ACU Press, 2001) 99.

7. Richard Hayes, *The Moral Vision Of The New Testament* (San Francisco: Harper Collins, 1996) 209-211.

8. Alice P. Matthews, *Discovering Biblical Equality*, 506.

9. Stackhouse, 31.

10. Iain W. Provan, "Why Bother With the Old Testament Regarding Gender and Sexuality" in *Christian Perspectives On Gender, Sexuality, and Community*, ed. by Maxine Hancock (Vancouver, British Columbia: Regent College Publishing, 2003) 33.

11. Gregory Sterling, "Women in the Hellenistic and Roman Worlds" and Randall D. Chestnutt, "Jewish Women in the Greco-Roman Era" in *Essays on Women in Earliest Christianity, volume 1*, ed. by Carroll D. Osburn (Abilene, Texas: ACU Press, 1993).

12. John Howard Yoder, *Body Politics* (Nashville: Discipleship Resources, 1989) 60.

13. Stackhouse, *Finally Feminist*, 30.

14. R.T. France, *Women in the Church's Ministry* (Eugene, Oregon: Wipf and Stock, 2004) 95.

15. William J. Webb, "A Redemptive Movement Hermeneutic" in *Discovering Biblical Equality*, 382-384.

16. Tom Wright, *Paul for Everyone, Galatians and Thessalonians* (Louisville: Westminster John Knox Press, 2004) 41-42.

17. Tom Wright, *Paul for Everyone, 1 Corinthians* (Louisville: John Knox Press, 2004) 139-143.

18. Iain Provan, 33.

19. Gordon Fee, *The First Epistle to the Corinthians* (Grand Rapids: William B. Eerdmans, 1987) 503.

20. Carroll Osburn, *Women in the Church*, 179.

21. Anthony C. Thiselton, *1 Corinthians* (Grand Rapids: William B. Eerdmans, 2006) 174.

22. Fee, 517.

23. Ibid., 524.

24. Wright, *1 Corinthians*, 141.

25. Thiselton, 173.

26. Kenneth B. Bailey, *Paul Through Mediterranean Eyes* (Grand Rapids: InterVarsity Press, 2011) 415-418.

27. McKnight, 164-165.

28. Stackhouse, 72.

29. Tom Wright, *Paul for Everyone, The Pastoral Letters* (London: Westminster John Knox Press, 2003) 25- 26.

30. Osburn, 243.

31. Wright, *The Pastoral Letters*, 23-27.

32. Osburn, 244.

33. Wright, *The Pastoral Letters*, 26.

34. Osburn, 249.

35. I. Howard Marshall, "The Gospel Does Not Change, But Our Perception of it May Need Revision" in *How I Changed My Mind About Women in Leadership*, ed. by Alan F. Johnson (Grand Rapids: Zondervan, 2010) 145.

36. Wright, *The Pastoral Letters*, 25.

37. McKnight, 202-204.

38. Osburn, 252.

39. Stackhouse, 53-55.

40. Ibid., 38-41.

41. McKnight, 205-207.

42. Stackhouse, 51.

43. Ibid., p. 56.

44. Ute E. Eisen, *Women Officeholders in Early Christianity* (Collegeville, Minnesota: Liturgical Press, 2000) VIII.

45. *Ordained Women in the Early Church*, ed. and translated by Kevin Madigan and Carolyn Isek (Baltimore: Johns Hopkins Press, 2005).

46. Stanley Grenz, *Women in the Church* (Downers Grove, Illinois: 1998) 36-45.

47. Peter Brown, *The Body and Society*, (New York: Columbia University Press, 1988) 9-10.

48. Donald Bloesch, *Is the Bible Sexist?* (Eugene, Oregon: Wipf and Stock, 2001).

49. Kathy J. Pulley, *Essays on Women in Earliest Christianity, Volume 11*, 460.

50. Osburn, 94.

51. Ibid.

52. Kevin Giles, "The Subordination of Christ and the Subordination of Women" in *Discovering Biblical Equality*, 334-340.

53. Chesterton, Internet site.

54. I. Howard Marshall, *Beyond the Bible* (Grand Rapids: Baker Academic, 2009) 79.

55. Thomas H. Olbricht, "Women in the Church: The Hermeneutical Problem" in *Essays on Women in Earliest Christianity, Volume 11*, 561-562.

56. Ibid.

57. Ibid., 554-561.

58. Osburn, *Women in the Church*, 266-267.

59. Thomas H. Olbricht, *Hearing God's Voice* (Abilene, TX: ACU Press, 1996) 289.

60. Olbricht, in *Essays on Women in Earliest Christianity, Volume 11*, 567.

61. Krister Stendahl, *The Bible and the Role of Women*, (Philadelphia: Fortress Press, 1966) 34.

62. France, 91.

63. Osburn, 267.

64. Ibid., 263.

65. Ibid., 265.

66. Stackhouse, *Finally Feminist*, 15-19.

67. Cornelius Plantinga, "How I Changed My Mind About Women in Church Leadership" in *How I Changed My Mind About Women in Church Leadership*, 194.

68. Ibid.

69. Ibid., 195.

70. Ibid.

71. Ibid.

72. Rodney Stark, *For the Glory of God* (Princeton, NJ: Princeton University Press, 2003) 345.

73. Ibid.

74. Ibid., 339.

75. Stanley N. Gundry, "From Bobbed Hair, Bossy Wives, and Women Preachers to Women Be Free: My Story" in *How I Changed My Mind*, 104.

76. William Webb, "A Redemptive-Movement Hermeneutic" in *Discovering Biblical Equality*, 38.

77. Dallas Willard, "Forward" in *How I Changed My Mind*, 10.

78. Ibid.

79. Bill Hybels, "Evangelicals and Biblical Equality," in *How My Mind Has Changed*, 110.

80. Ibid., Willard, 11.

81. John Stackhouse, *Evangelical Landscapes* (Grand Rapids: Baker Academic, 2002) 37-45.

82. Don Browning, "The Problem of Men" in *Does Christianity Teach Male Headship?* ed. by David Blankenhorn, Don Browning, and Mary Stewart Van Leeuwen (Grand Rapids: William B. Eerdmans, 2004) 9, 11.

83. James Thompson, "The Submission of Wives in 1 Peter," in *Essays on Women in Earliest Christianity, Volume 11*, ed. by Carroll D. Osburn (Joplin, MO: College Press, 1993) 392.

84. Browning, 5.

85. Browning, 6-7.

86. James Thompson, 377-393.

87. C.S. Lewis, *A Grief Observed*, (New York: Seabury Press, 1961) 57-58.

Made in the USA
Middletown, DE
06 June 2016